# Windows 3.1
## The Visual Learning Guide

Watch for these forthcoming titles in this series:

Excel 4 for Windows: The Visual Learning Guide
Word for Windows 2: The Visual Learning Guide
1-2-3 for Windows: The Visual Learning Guide
WordPerfect for Windows: The Visual Learning Guide

**How to Order:**

Quantity discounts are available from the publisher, Prima Publishing, P.O. Box 1260 WIN, Rocklin, CA 95677; telephone (916) 786-0449. On your letterhead include information concerning the intended use of the books and the number of books you wish to purchase.

# Windows 3.1
## The Visual Learning Guide

David C. Gardner, Ph.D.

Grace Joely Beatty, Ph.D.

Prima Publishing
P.O. Box 1260 WIN
Rocklin, CA 95677
(916) 786-0426

Managing Editor: Roger Stewart
Project Manager: Laurie Stewart
Production: Marian Hartsough Associates and Matt Kim
Interior Design: Grace Joely Beatty and S. Linda Beatty with help from Lisa Anderson, Tom Kordis, and David C. Gardner
Graphic Design: Grace Joely Beatty, David C. Gardner, and S. Linda Beatty
Technical Editing: Harriet Serenkin
Copyediting: Chet Bell
Cover Design: Kirschner-Caroff Design
Color Separations: Ocean Quigley
Index: Katherine Stimson

Prima Publishing
Rocklin, CA 95677-1260

Every effort has been made to supply complete and accurate information. However, neither the publisher nor the authors assume any responsibility for its use, nor for any infringements of patents or other rights of third parties that would result.

**Library of Congress Cataloging-in-Publication Data**

Gardner, David C., 1934–
Windows 3.1: the visual learning guide / David C. Gardner and Grace Joely Beatty
      p. cm. — (Prima visual learning guides)
Includes index.
ISBN 1-55958-182-4: $19.95
1. Microsoft Windows (Computer program)  I. Beatty, Grace Joely
1947–    .    II. Title.    III. Series
QA76.76.W56B43 1992
005.4′3—dc20                  9143913
                                  CIP

92 93 94 95 RRD 10 9 8 7 6 5 4 3 2
Printed in the United States of America

# Acknowledgments

We would like to thank those who have contributed to this book and the series in so many ways.

Bill Gladstone of Waterside Productions whose faith in us never wavered and who, with Matt Wagner, created the idea for this series.

Roger Stewart, our editor sine qua non, beta tester, screen capturer, and marketeer. A man of many talents!

Laurie Stewart, our project manager and an author's dream.

Harriet Serenkin who is a terrific technical editor and lots of fun to work with!

Joseph and Shirley Beatty without whom there would be no series.

Asher Schapiro who has always been there when we needed him.

Carolyn Holder who not only struggled through the first draft of every chapter but who also served as daily therapist and proofreader par excellence.

Linda Beatty who worked incredible hours under pressure and still managed to create wonderful "designerly" graphics and templates for the entire series. We could not have done it without her!

Paula Gardner Capaldo and David Capaldo who have always supported our dream; Joshua and Jessica Gardner for being terrific kids. A special thanks to Stephen Capaldo.

We worked with numerous reviewers who gave generously of their time so that others like them could master 3.1. We cannot thank them enough: Carolyn and Ray Holder, Tom and Maura Healy, Lisa Anderson, David A. Coburn, Nancy Norkunas, Will Schiefer, and Joseph and Shirley Beatty.

We could not have kept the ball rolling without the following technical support: Fred Harper of Dymerc International, Jerry Hayward of Gazelle Systems, Glen Horton of Inner Media, Inc., Michael Ayotte of Applications Techniques, Inc., Linda Miles, and Michael Daschuk of Corel Draw.

Thank you all!

For

BLAIR

# Contents at a Glance

# CONTENTS

## Part II: Customizing Windows

## Part III: Printing

# Part V: Using Windows Programs

# Customize Your Learning

Prima Visual Learning Guides are not like any other computer books you have ever seen. They are based on our years in the classroom, our corporate consulting, and our research at Boston University on the best ways to teach technical information to nontechnical learners. Most important, this series is based on the feedback of a panel of reviewers who range in computer knowledge from "panicked at the thought" to very sophisticated.

This is not an everything-you've-ever-wanted-to-know-about-Windows 3.1-but-didn't-know-enough-to-ask book. It is designed to give you the information you need to perform basic (and some not-so-basic) functions with confidence and skill. It is a book that our reviewers claim makes it "really easy" for anyone to learn Windows 3.1 quickly.

Each chapter is illustrated with full-color screen shots to guide you through every task. The combination of screens, step-by-step instructions, and pointers make it impossible for you to get lost or confused as you follow along on your own computer. You can either work through from the beginning to the end or skip around to master the skills you need. If you have a specific goal you want to accomplish now, choose it from the following section.

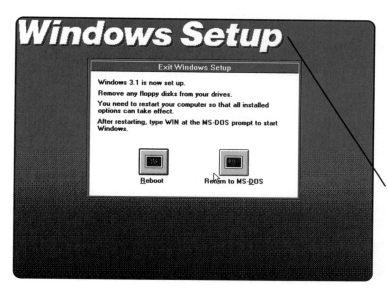

## SELECT YOUR GOALS

❖ I would like help installing Windows 3.1.

Go to Appendix A, "Installing for First-Time and Upgrade Users."

❖ I'm new to Windows and would like help getting started.

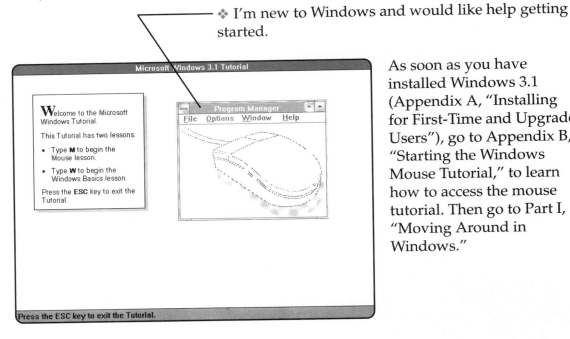

As soon as you have installed Windows 3.1 (Appendix A, "Installing for First-Time and Upgrade Users"), go to Appendix B, "Starting the Windows Mouse Tutorial," to learn how to access the mouse tutorial. Then go to Part I, "Moving Around in Windows."

❖ I want to know how to set up and customize my desktop so that the programs I use most will be located in one place.

Go to Part II, "Customizing Windows."

❖ I want to know how to have several programs running at the same time (*multitasking*).

Go to Chapter 3, "Working with Multiple Programs."

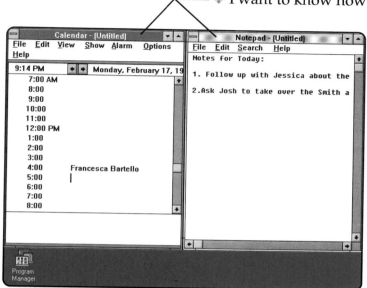

❖ I want to install a printer and learn how to print.

Windows 3.1 will automatically install your printer during its installation. Later, you can change or add a printer by following the instructions in Chapter 12, "Changing Your Primary Printer." Also, go to Chapter 13, "Basic Printer Settings," to learn how to get your printer working smoothly in Windows. For additional information on printing, see Chapters 14 to 17 in Part III.

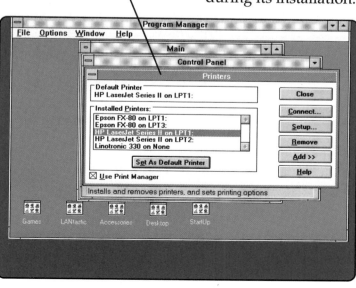

❖ I want to install additional fonts that were not included in the basic Windows 3.1 installation.

Go to Chapter 14, "Installing Fonts."

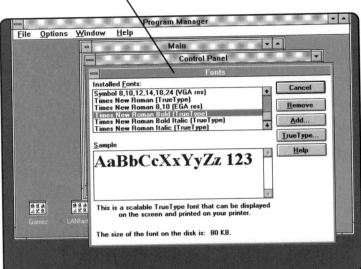

❖ I want to learn how to use the two basic word processing programs that are included with Windows 3.1. I would also like to know how to use the Windows Clock feature.

Go to Part V, "Using Windows Programs."

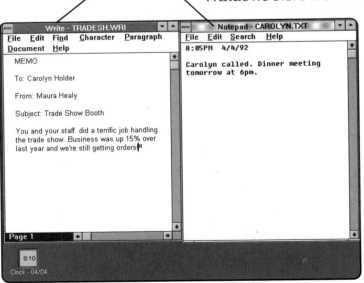

❖ I would like to learn how to organize my document files.

Go to Chapter 18, "An Overview of File Manager," to learn how to view file information and copy, delete, and move files.

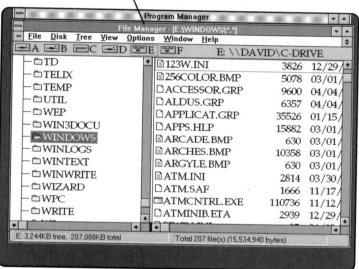

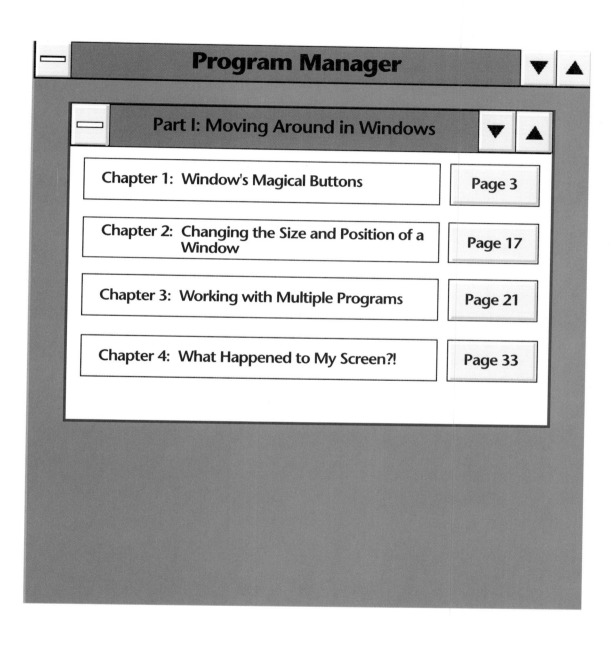

# Windows' Magical Buttons

If you are new to the Windows environment you will find you can manipulate what you see on your screen in ways that at first may seem almost magical. You can reduce programs to tiny pictures (icons), then enlarge them again at the click of a button. You can use the mouse to move around on the screen quickly and easily. And you can perform most functions in a variety of ways. In this chapter you will:

❖ Learn several different ways to open and close windows

❖ Learn several different ways to minimize a window to an icon, restore the icon to window size, and maximize the window to fill the screen completely

❖ Use scroll bars to move around within a window

## STARTING UP WINDOWS

1. **Type win** after the C:\> prompt. This will start (*boot up*) the Windows program and open the Windows Program Manager on your screen.

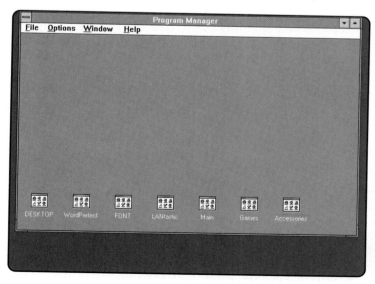

Depending on how Windows was installed on your computer, you may have different group icons at the bottom of your screen than the ones you see here. You will, however, have the Main and Accessories icons mentioned in this chapter. In the first three sections you will use three different methods of opening a group window.

3

# OPENING A GROUP WINDOW: METHOD #1

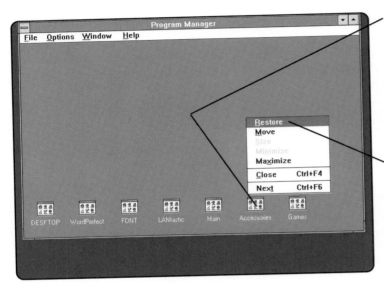

1. **Click once** on the **Accessories group icon** at the bottom of your screen. (It may be in a different spot than you see here.) A pop-up control menu will appear.

2. **Click on Restore**. The Accessories group icon will become a window. Notice that it contains icons for different programs.

# OPENING A GROUP WINDOW: METHOD #2

In this section you will open a second window and lay it over the Accessories group window.

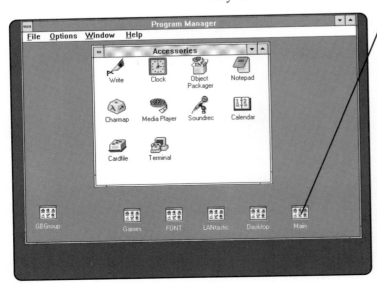

1. **Click twice** on the **Main group icon** at the bottom of your screen. (It may take a little practice to get the right rhythm on the double-clicks.) The icon will become a window and will be placed on top of the Accessories group window. The Main group window may be a different size and in a different location than the way it looks in the next section.

# OPENING A GROUP WINDOW: METHOD #3

You will now open a third window and lay it over the previous two.

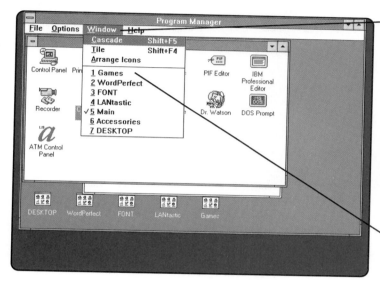

1. **Click** on **Window** in the menu bar. A pull-down menu that contains the names of your group windows will appear.

Notice that Main, which is the *active window* (the window in which you are currently working), has a check mark beside it.

2. **Click** on **Games**. It will become a window and be placed on top of the two windows on your screen.

# MINIMIZING A WINDOW: METHOD #1

In this and the next section you will learn two ways to minimize windows.

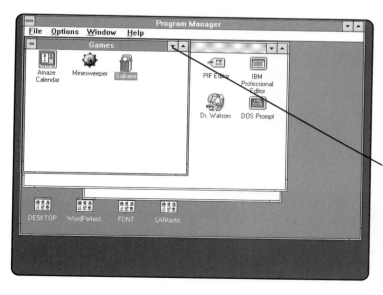

1. **Click** on the **Minimize button (▼)** on the right side of the Games group window title bar. The Games group window will be reduced to an icon at the bottom of your screen.

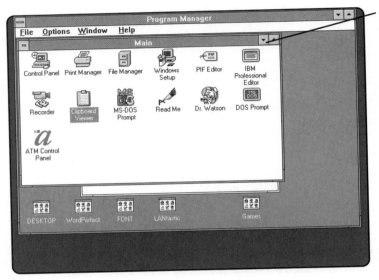

2. **Click** on the **Minimize button (▼)** on the right side of the Main group window title bar. The Main group window will be minimized to an icon at the bottom of your screen.

# MINIMIZING A WINDOW: METHOD #2

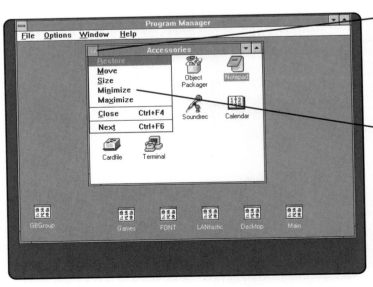

1. **Click** on the **Control menu box** in the left corner of the Accessories group window title bar. A pull-down menu will appear.

2. **Click** on **Minimize**. The Accessories group window will be minimized to an icon at the bottom of your screen.

# ALIGNING ICONS USING THE MOUSE

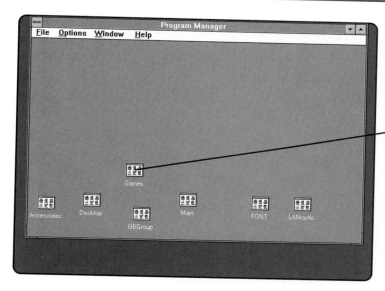

If your icons have gotten out of alignment you can arrange them in any pattern you wish using the mouse.

1. **Move** the mouse arrow to an **icon**.

2. **Press and hold** the mouse button as you **drag** the **icon** to a new spot.

3. **Release** the mouse button when the icon is where you want it to be.

# ALIGNING ICONS AUTOMATICALLY

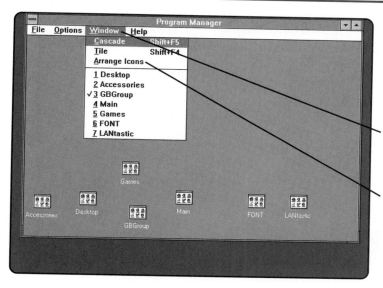

Use this method to arrange the icons automatically. However, you have no control over where they are placed.

1. **Click** on **Windows** in the menu bar. A pull-down menu will appear.

2. **Click** on **Arrange Icons**. The icons will be arranged automatically in a straight row.

# MAXIMIZING A WINDOW: METHOD #1

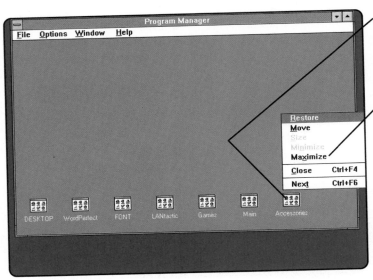

1. **Click once** on the **Accessories group icon**. A pop-up control menu will appear.

2. **Click** on **Maximize**. The Accessories group window will be enlarged to its maximum size.

# RESTORING A WINDOW: METHOD #1

Notice that the name of the maximized window appears in the Program Manager title bar. Also, the group icons at the bottom of the desktop space are hidden behind the maximized window.

1. **Click** on the **Restore button** on the right side of the menu bar. The Accessories group window will appear in its standard size. The only time you will see a Restore button is when a window is in its maximized form.

# MAXIMIZING A WINDOW: METHOD #2

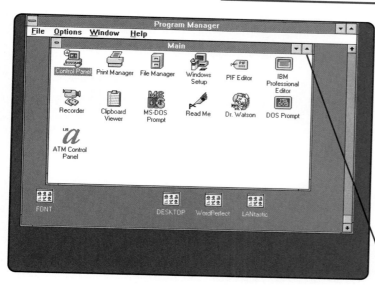

**1. Click twice** on the **Main group icon** at the bottom of your screen. If you don't click quickly enough the pop-up menu will appear. It's okay if that happens. Simply click on Restore. The Main group will appear in window size on your screen and overlay the Accessories group window.

**2. Click** on the **Maximize button (▲)** on the right of the Main group window title bar. The window will be enlarged to its maximum size. The Accessories group window is hidden behind it.

# RESTORING A WINDOW: METHOD #2

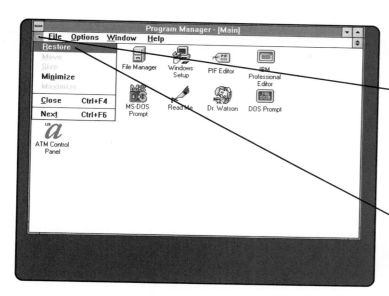

**1. Click** on the **Control menu box** in the menu bar. A pull-down menu will appear. Be careful not to click on the Control menu box for Program Manager.

**2. Click** on **Restore**. The Main group window will be restored to its former (standard) size.

# CLOSING A GROUP WINDOW: METHOD #1

Group windows never actually close. They shrink and remain in icon form at the bottom of your screen. The only way to remove a group window from your screen is to delete it. (See the section "Deleting a Group Icon" in Chapter 6.) You can close, or shrink, a group icon in two ways.

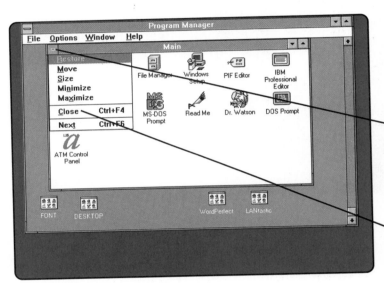

1. **Click** on the **Control menu box** on the left of the Main group window title bar. A pull-down menu will appear.

2. **Click** on **Close**. The window will be minimized to an icon.

# CLOSING A GROUP WINDOW: METHOD #2

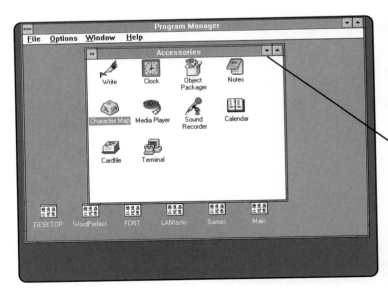

1. **Click** on the **Minimize button (▼)** on the right of the Accessories group window title bar.

The window will be minimized to an icon at the bottom of your screen.

# USING SCROLL BARS

Scroll bars help you move around within a window.

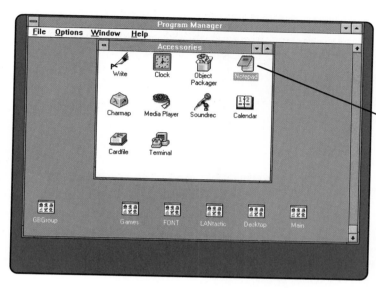

1. **Click twice** on the **Accessories group icon**. It will be restored to window size.

2. **Click twice** on the **Notepad icon**. The Notepad window with a new file opened will appear on your screen.

It may appear in a different size or location than you see below.

Scroll bars are at the right edge and at the bottom edge of the Notepad window.

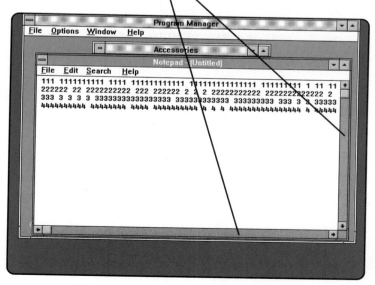

Text was typed into the Notepad file so you could see how the scroll bars affect what you see of the screen. Enter four lines of text into the Notepad file on your screen if you want to follow along with these steps and see changes on your screen. Press the Enter key when you want to start a new line of type.

# SCROLLING ONE LINE AT A TIME

**1. Click** on the **scroll down arrow** on the right scroll bar (called the *vertical scroll bar*) to move down one line. Click once for every line you want to move down. This example shows a view where the scroll down arrow was clicked twice.

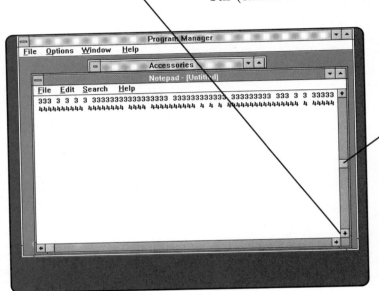

Notice the scroll box has moved to the middle of the scroll bar. As you scroll down the file the scroll box will show where you are in the file. Since this file has only four lines of text, scrolling down two lines brings you half way through the file.

**2. Click** on the **scroll up arrow** on the scroll bar to move up in the file. This example shows a view where the up arrow was clicked to bring the first line into view.

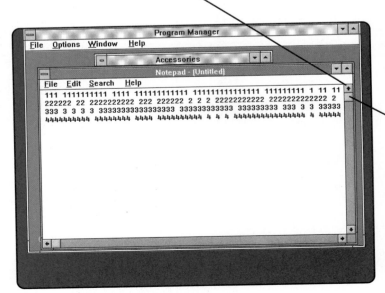

Notice that the scroll box has moved to the top of the scroll bar to reflect that you are at the beginning of the file.

When you are at the top of the file, clicking on the scroll up arrow will have no effect.

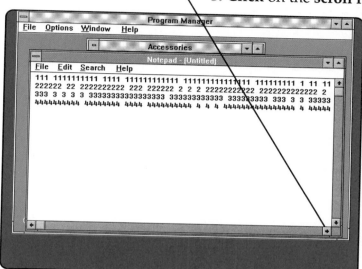

3. **Click** on the **scroll right arrow** on the bottom scroll bar (called the *horizontal scroll bar*) to move to the right.

This example shows a view where the arrow has been clicked several times.

Notice that the scroll box has moved to the right on the bar.

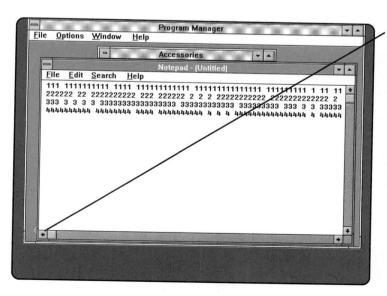

4. **Click** on the **scroll left arrow** to move back to the left.

Notice that the scroll box has moved to the far left on the bar to reflect that you are at the left margin of your file.

# SCROLLING RAPIDLY: METHOD #1

**1. Click** to the **left or right** of the scroll box on the bottom scroll bar to move rapidly to the left or right.

**2. Click above or below** the scroll box on the right scroll bar to move up or down rapidly.

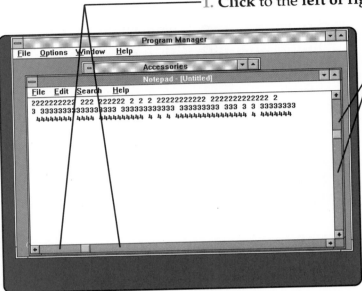

# SCROLLING RAPIDLY: METHOD #2

**1. Press and hold** any **scroll arrow**. This will move you rapidly through the file in the direction of the arrow.

# SCROLLING TO ANY POSITION

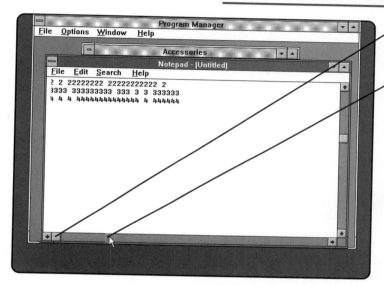

**1. Move** the mouse arrow to the **bottom scroll box**.

**2. Press and hold** the mouse button as you **drag** the **arrow** across the bar.

If you drag slowly you will see an outline of the scroll box being dragged across the bar. The scroll box itself will not move.

**3. Release** the mouse button when you have moved the screen to the position you want to see. The scroll box will appear at the spot where you released the mouse button. The scroll box on the vertical scroll bar works the same way.

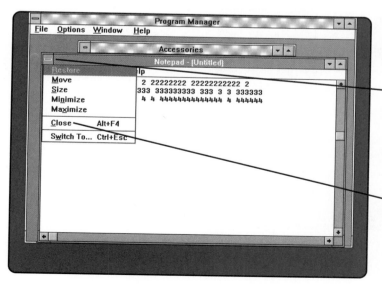

# CLOSING A PROGRAM

**1. Click** on the **Control menu box** in the left corner of the Notepad title bar. A pull-down menu will appear.

**2. Click** on **Close**. The Notepad dialog box will appear.

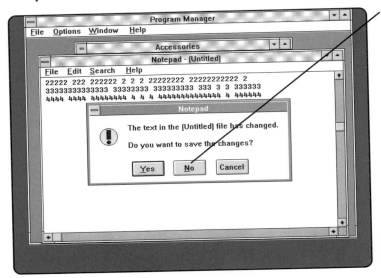

3. **Click** on **No**. This will close the Notepad file without saving the material you typed.

# CLOSING A GROUP WINDOW: METHOD #3

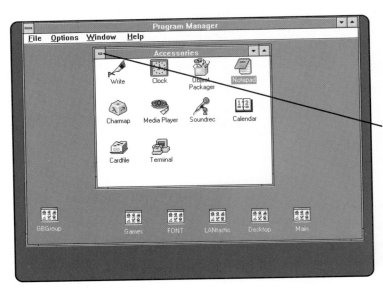

There are many ways to do the same procedure in Windows. Here is yet another way to close a window.

1. **Click twice** on the **Control menu box** on the left of the Accessories title bar. The window will close and be minimized to an icon.

# Changing the Size and Position of a Window

## CHAPTER 2

You have tremendous control over how things look on your screen when you work in Windows. In this chapter you will:

❖ Change the size of a window
❖ Move a window to another location on your screen

## CHANGING THE SIZE OF A WINDOW

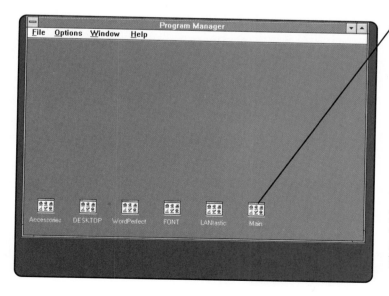

1. **Click twice** on the **Main group icon** at the bottom of your screen. The Main group window will be restored to window size.

Depending on how Windows was installed on your computer, you may have different group icons from the ones you see here. Also, they may be in a different order at the bottom of your screen.

2. **Move** the mouse arrow to the **right edge** of the Main group window. (If the Main group window appears to the far right on your screen, move the mouse arrow to the left edge of the window.) The mouse arrow will change to a two-headed arrow. You may have to fiddle with the position of the mouse arrow to get it to change to the two-headed arrow.

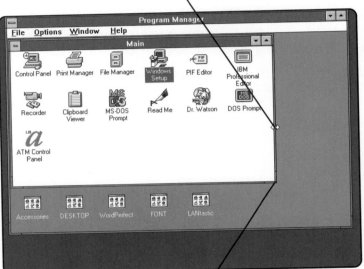

3. **Press and hold** the mouse button as you drag the edge of the window to the right (or left) to enlarge it.

4. **Release** the mouse button when the window is the size you want. Notice that the icons are automatically rearranged as the space in the window changes.

If you drag the right or left edge, the window changes in width. If you drag the bottom edge, the window changes in height.

If you want to change both the width and height at the same time, position the mouse arrow on a corner.

You can do these procedures to make a window larger or smaller.

You can enlarge or reduce the size of most windows. However, some application windows, such as Control Panel, have a fixed size.

# CHANGING THE POSITION OF A WINDOW

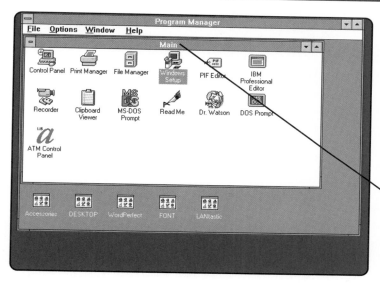

If you have been following the steps in this chapter, the Main group window is on your screen and enlarged.

In this section, you will move the Main group window to the center of your screen.

**1. Move** the mouse arrow to the **title bar** of the Main group window. (Unlike the previous section, "Changing the Size of a Window," the arrow does not change shape in this procedure.)

**2. Press and hold** the mouse button as you **drag** the **Main group window** to the center of the screen. You will see an outline of the window being dragged.

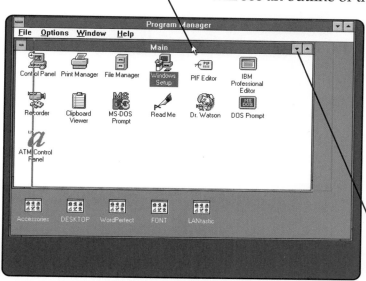

**Release** the mouse button when the outline is where you want the window to be. The window will appear in place of the outline.

You can change the position of group windows, program windows, and dialog boxes —almost anything that has a title bar.

**3.** Click on the **Minimize button (▼)** to close the Main group window.

# Working with Multiple Programs

The ability to have multiple software programs on your screen at the same time (multitasking) is a major feature of Windows. As with most other Windows functions, there are several ways in which you can do this. In this chapter you will:

❖ Minimize several programs to icons and switch back and forth between them

❖ Have several programs on your screen in a cascade setup

❖ Have several programs on your screen in a tile setup

## MINIMIZING A PROGRAM WINDOW TO AN ICON

In this section you will open two programs (software applications). You will minimize each program to an icon at the bottom of your screen, and switch back and forth between them. The following examples involve the Calendar and Notepad programs that come with Windows. You can, however, use these procedures with any program that works in Windows.

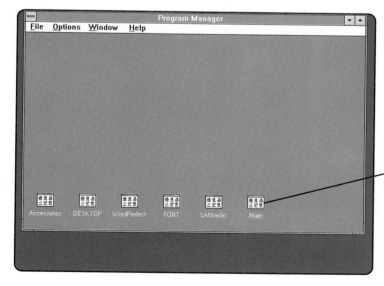

1. **Click twice** on the **Accessories group icon** at the bottom of the Program Manager screen. The Accessories group window will appear on your screen.

**21**

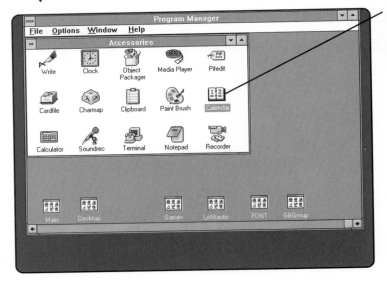

2. **Click twice** on the **Calendar icon**. The Calendar program will appear on your screen.

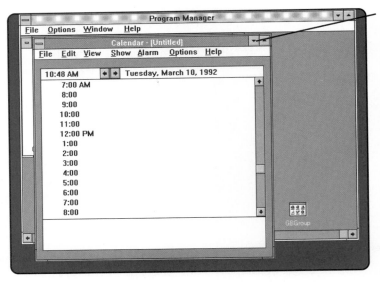

3. **Click on the Minimize button** (▼) in the Calendar title bar. (Be careful not to click on the Minimize button in the Accessories title bar.) Calendar will be minimized to an icon at the bottom of your screen.

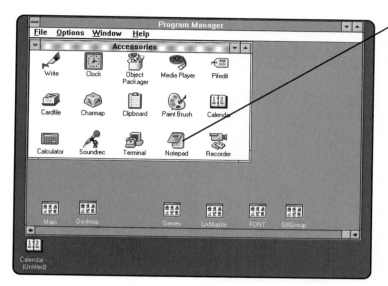

**4. Click twice** on the **Notepad icon.** The Notepad program will appear on your screen.

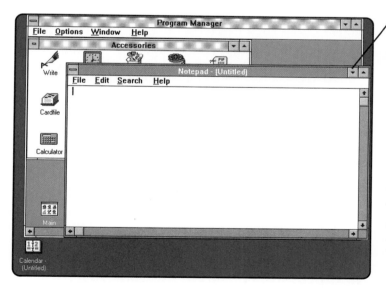

**5. Click** on the **Minimize button (▼)** in the Notepad title bar. Notepad will be minimized to an icon at the bottom of your screen.

You don't have to minimize a program at the opening screen. You can do it at any time, even while you are working in a specific file in the program.

# SWITCHING BETWEEN PROGRAMS

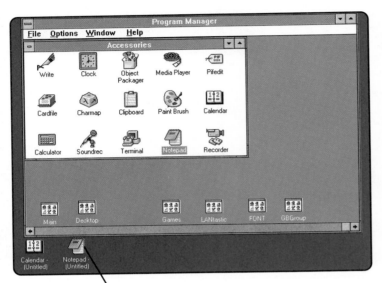

Programs that you use frequently during the day can be kept at the bottom of your screen. For example, if you keep Calendar in icon form at the bottom of your screen, it is available at the double-click of your mouse. You don't have to close the program in which you are currently working to have access to Calendar. You don't even have to minimize the current program. Just click twice on the Calendar icon. It will become a window that is laid over whatever program is on your screen. Make entries you want in Calendar (and save the changes, of course). Then minimize Calendar when you are through with it. The program in which you were working will still be on your screen when you minimize Calendar. Try this with the two programs you minimized in this section:

1. **Click twice** on the **Notepad icon** at the bottom of your screen. The program will be restored to a window.

This example shows that work has been done in the Notepad file. It's not necessary for you to actually enter data into the Notepad file to follow these steps, however. Assume that while you are working in this file you receive a telephone call that requires you to consult your calendar.

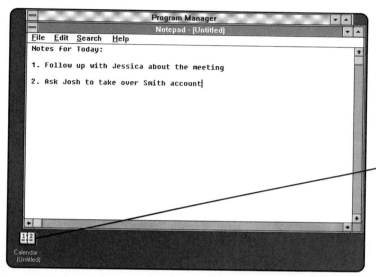

**2. Click twice** on the **Calendar icon** at the bottom of your screen. It will be restored to a window and be placed over the Notepad file.

You can now work in the Calendar program without affecting the Notepad data. When you are through with the Calendar:

**3. Click** on the **Minimize button** (▼) to the right of the Calendar title bar. It will be minimized to an icon and the Notepad will show on your screen. You can switch back and forth between programs as many times as you want.

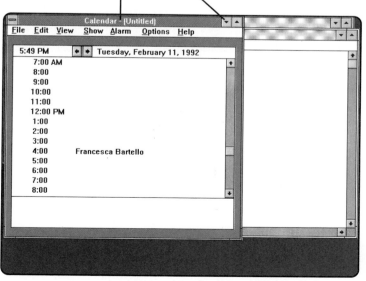

The following sections describe other methods of working with multiple programs. In preparation for the next section, **click** on the **Minimize button** (▼) on the right of the Notepad title bar. Notepad will be minimized to an icon at the bottom of the screen.

# CASCADING MULTIPLE PROGRAM WINDOWS

If you have not already done so, open the Calendar and Notepad programs (in the Accessories group window) and minimize them to icons at the bottom of your screen. See the earlier section in this chapter, "Minimizing a Program Window to an Icon," if you need help. If you have been following along with this chapter, you have already done these steps.

When you tell Windows to cascade, it arranges all programs that are window-sized in an overlapping cascade. It will not arrange a program that has been minimized to an icon.

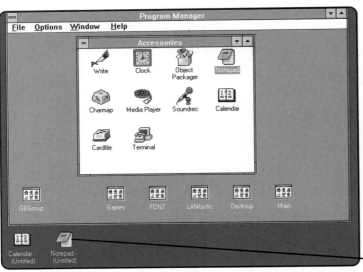

**1.** **Click twice** on the **Notepad icon**. It will be restored to full window size and placed over the Accessories window on the Program Manager screen.

**2.** **Click twice** on the **Calendar icon**.

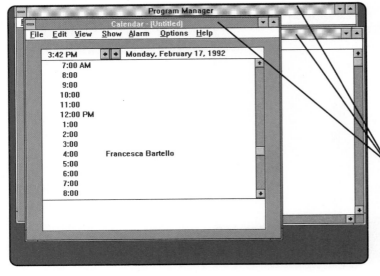

It will be restored to full window size and placed over the Notepad program and the Program Manager screen.

3. **Press and hold** the **Ctrl** key while you **press** the **Esc** key (Ctrl + Esc). The Task List dialog box will appear. The Task List shows all programs that are currently running. The active program (in this example, Calendar) is highlighted. Notice that Program Manager is listed. Although it is not an application program, it runs Windows and is, therefore, always included in the Task List. If you close Program Manager, you close Windows.

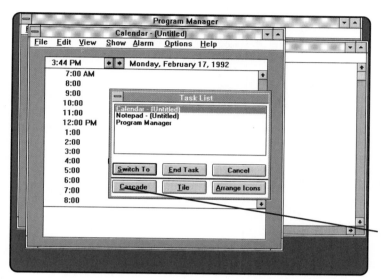

4. **Click** on **Cascade**. The three windows will be arranged in a cascade setup.

In a cascade the active window is in the front. The other windows are in the background. The title bar of the active window is dark. The title bars of the other windows are dimmed. The exact colors of the active and inactive title bars depend on the color scheme you choose. See Chapter 9, "Customizing Colors and Patterns."

Use the scroll bars to move within the active window.

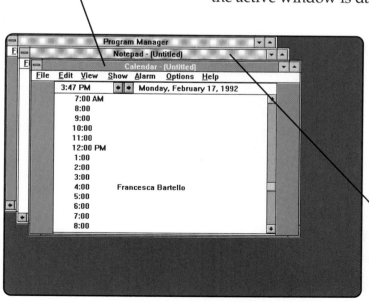

5. **Click anywhere** on one of the **background windows** to make it the active window. It will move to the front and the other programs will be in the background.

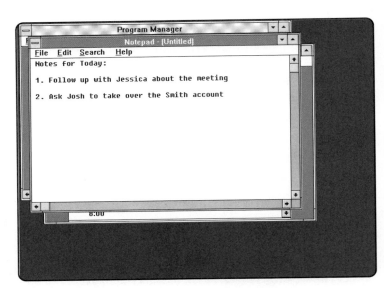

You can move back and forth between programs by clicking anywhere on the window in which you want to work. It will be brought to the foreground and the other two will be in the background.

After several clicks you may find that a window is difficult to see. You can move the windows to different places on the screen. See Chapter 2, "Changing the Size and Position of a Window."

## TILING MULTIPLE PROGRAMS

In a tile setup, Windows will resize the program windows to fit side by side on your screen. Since Windows will include all programs that are window-sized in the tile setup, it is best to minimize Program Manager so it will not take up space on the screen.

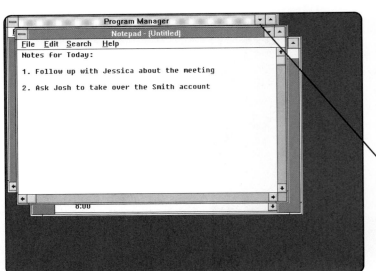

1. **Click** on the **Minimize button (▼)** on the right of the Program Manager title bar. It will be minimized to an icon at the bottom of the screen.

**2. Click twice** on a **clear spot** on the screen. The Task List dialog box will appear. (This is another way to bring up the Task List.)

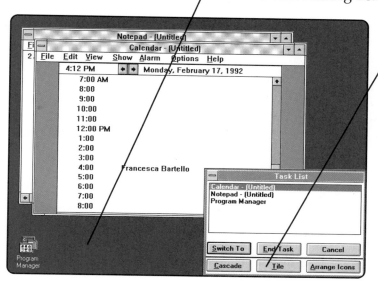

**3. Click on Tile**. The Calendar and the Notepad will be arranged side by side on the screen.

The colored title bar in Calendar indicates that it is the active window. You can move around in the active window with the scroll bars.

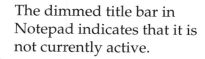

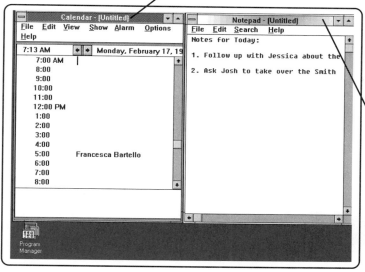

The dimmed title bar in Notepad indicates that it is not currently active.

**4. Click** on the **title bar** in Notepad to make it the active program. The title bar will change to a brighter color and the title bar of Calendar will become dimmed.

# CLOSING PROGRAMS WITH TASK LIST

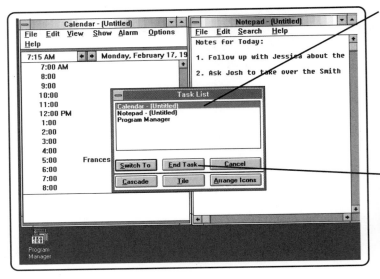

1. **Press and hold** the **Ctrl** key while you **press** the **Esc** key (Ctrl + Esc). The Task List dialog box will appear.

Notice that Calendar is the active (highlighted) program.

2. **Click** on **End Task**. If you did not enter anything into Calendar during this exercise, it will close and disappear from the screen. If you entered anything into Calendar, a message box will appear.

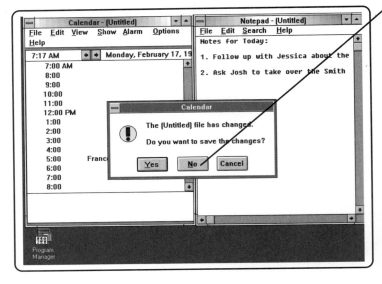

3. **Click** on **No**. The program will close and the data entered will not be saved.

If you click on Yes, a dialog box will appear and ask for the name under which you want to save the file.

If you click on Cancel, the End Task command is canceled and Calendar will be back on your screen.

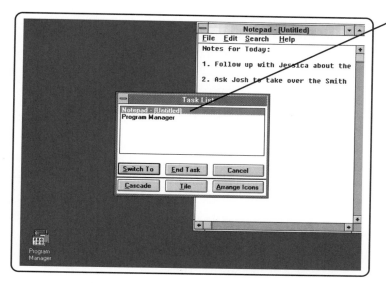

**4.** Confirm that Notepad is highlighted (selected).

**5. Repeat steps 1 to 3** to close Notepad.

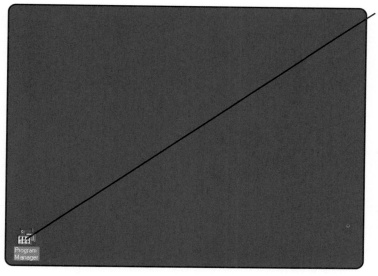

**6. Click twice** on the **Program Manager icon**. It will be restored to window size. The Accessories group window will be on the screen.

**7. Click** on the **Minimize button (▼)** on the right of the Accessories group window title bar. It will be minimized to an icon at the bottom of your screen.

# What Happened to My Screen?!

Windows is an amazingly flexible program. As you have seen in Chapters 1, 2, and 3, you have a great deal of control over how your screen looks. There are times, however, when you may feel you have no control. Programs suddenly vanish. Or, they move around on your screen as if they have lives of their own. It can be very frustrating to say the least!

The good news is that the solutions to these mysteries are fairly straightforward. In this chapter you will:

❖ See common situations in which strange things happen to the screen. You can compare these to situations in which you may find (or have found) yourself

❖ See a number of possible solutions that you can try on your own

## THE CASE OF THE DISAPPEARING PROGRAM

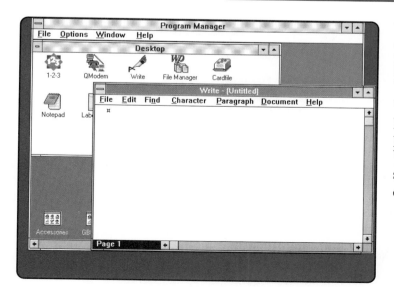

You click on something on your screen and the program in which you are working suddenly disappears! There are three possible solutions to this problem. In this example, Windows Write is on your screen and suddenly disappears.

# Solution #1

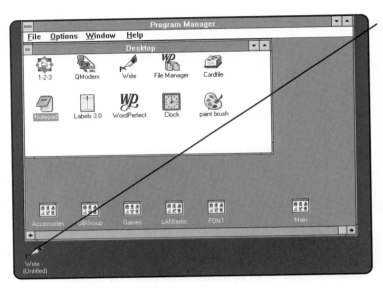

1. Check to see if the program is in icon form at the bottom of your screen.

If it is, you mistakenly clicked on the Minimize button (▼) in the program title bar.

2. **Click twice** on the **Write icon** at the bottom of the screen to restore the program to window size.

# Solution #2

1. Check to see if a piece of the program is sticking out from behind Program Manager, either from the side or from the bottom.

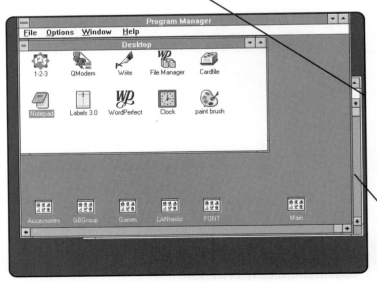

If it is, you mistakenly clicked on a part of the Program Manager or Desktop screen. Windows considers this a command to bring Program Manager to the foreground and send the current program to the background.

2. **Click** on **any part** of the **program** that is sticking out. It will be returned to the foreground.

# Solution #3

If your program is nowhere to be seen, the easiest way to figure out what is happening is to bring up the Task List dialog box. The Task List dialog box will include all programs that are currently running, even if they are not visible on your screen.

1. **Click twice** on a **clear place** on the screen. Or, if there is no clear space, **press and hold** the **Ctrl** key then **press** the **Esc** key (Ctrl + Esc). The Task List dialog box will appear.

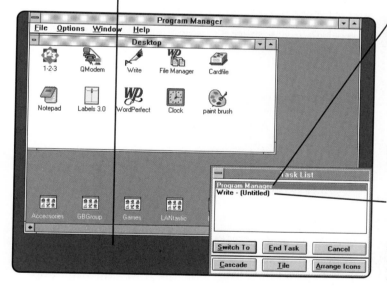

The highlight bar tells you that Program Manager is the active program. Program Manager will always appear on the Task List because it runs Windows. If you close Program Manager, you close Windows.

Write is also running. The fact that you can't see it on the screen means it is hidden behind the Program Manager window.

Even though Desktop appears on your screen, it is not listed as a program in the Task List dialog box. That is because Desktop is a *group* window. It holds icons for different programs but is not itself an application.

Desktop is a customized group window. See Chapter 5, "Setting Up Your Windows Programs and Groups," for directions on how to set up a customized group window.

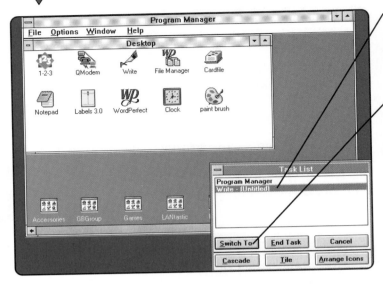

**2. Click** on the **program** you want to be active. (In this example, it is Write.) It will be highlighted.

**3. Click** on **Switch To**. The Write program will appear on your screen.

# THE CASE OF THE DISAPPEARING ICONS

When your group icons disappear, there are several possible solutions.

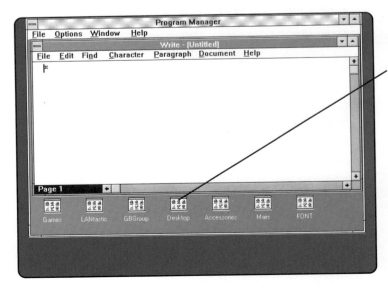

## Solution #1

In this first example, you are working in the Write program. You have a number of group icons at the bottom of your screen. You do something that makes the Write program suddenly become very large and the icons at the bottom of your screen disappear.

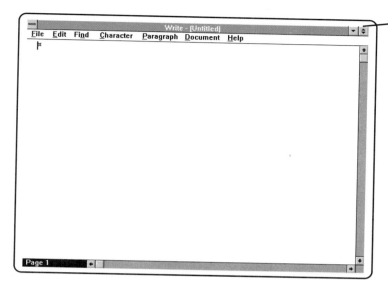

1. Check to see if the Restore button is on the right of the title bar. This appears only when a window is in its maximized form. If it is there, you mistakenly clicked on the Maximize (▲) button in the title bar when the program was in standard size. That button maximizes the size of the window to fill the screen. The maximized window will cover the icons at the bottom of the screen.

2. **Click** on the **Restore button**. The Write window will be restored to standard size and the icons will be visible.

# Solution #2

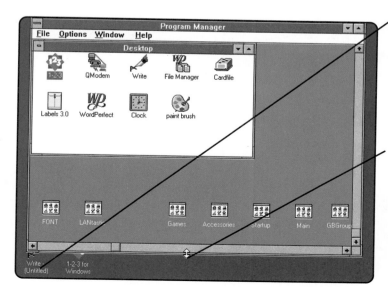

Sometimes the Program Manager window hides programs that have been minimized to icons, such as the two programs in this example.

1. **Reduce** the size of the **Program Manager window** by dragging the bottom of the window up. This will bring the program icons into view. See "Changing the Size of a Window" in Chapter 2 if you need help.

# WHEN ALL ELSE FAILS

Sometimes the arrangement of windows on your screen becomes so confusing that you just are not able to restore it to the arrangement you prefer. In that case, try this "quick fix."

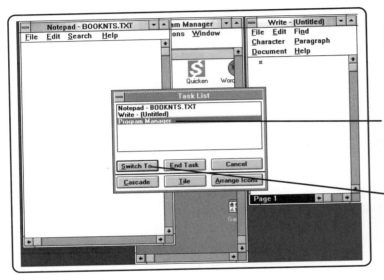

1. **Press and hold** the **Ctrl** key and **press** the **Esc** key (Ctrl + Esc). This will bring up the Task List dialog box.

2. **Click** on **Program Manager**. It will be highlighted.

3. **Click** on **Switch To**. Program Manager will come to the foreground.

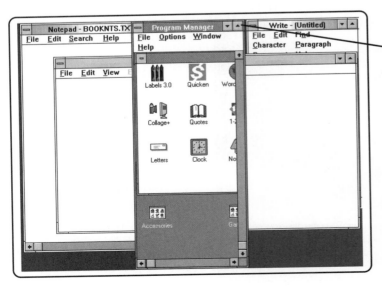

4. **Click** on the **Maximize button (▲)** on the right of the Program Manager title bar. Program Manager will be maximized to fill the screen.

5. **Click** on **Options** in the menu bar. A pull-down menu will appear.

6. **Click** on **Save Settings on Exit** to remove the check mark. If there is no check mark, click anywhere outside of the pull-down menu. The pull-down menu will disappear.

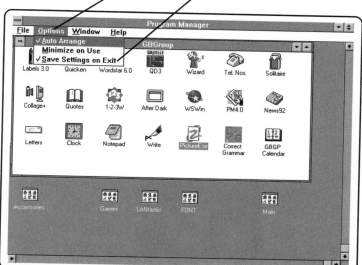

7. **Press and hold** the **Alt** key while you **press** the **F4** key (Alt + F4). This is the command to exit Windows.

You will see a message box with the statement, "This will end your Windows session."

8. **Click** on **OK**.

Don't worry if you didn't save before you started the exit process. Windows will ask if you want to save changes in any program that is open.

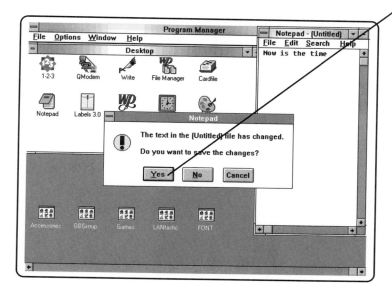

9. **Click** on **Yes** to save any changes made in the file. Windows will close and you will be at the DOS prompt.

10. **Type win** at the C:\>. When Windows appears on your screen, your original settings will be restored. You may want to reopen the Options pull-down menu and click on Save Settings on Exit to ensure that your settings are saved the next time you exit Windows.

# Program Manager

## Part II: Customizing Windows

# Setting Up Your Windows Programs and Groups

Before converting to Windows, you probably worked with programs designed for DOS. DOS is a text-based, rather than a graphics-based, way of interacting with your computer. You may have had a menu from which you launched your programs by pressing a number or a letter on your keyboard. In Windows you launch programs by clicking on an icon that represents the program. To do this, you need a place to store the program icons until you are ready to use them. Windows calls these storage areas groups. In this chapter you will:

❖ Make a customized group window that will serve as your major work area in Windows

❖ Transfer your most-used program icons to this customized group window

## ADVANTAGES OF A CUSTOMIZED GROUP WINDOW

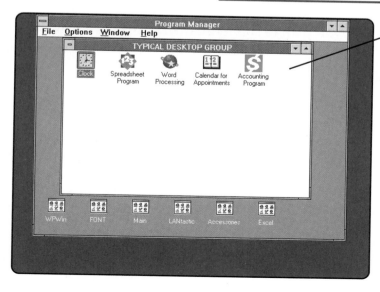

This is a "bare bones" illustration of a customized group window. For an overview of a customized group window turn to the next page.

This illustration of a customized group window represents programs the average person might use during the course of the day.

This customized group window contains five programs icons:

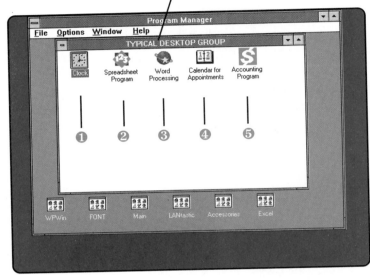

❶ The Windows Clock program

❷ A spreadsheet program

❸ A word processing program

❹ A calendar program for keeping appointments

❺ An accounting program.

The advantages of a customized group window are:

❖ All of your most-used programs are in one place. This means they are immediately available.

❖ If you plan to run more than one program at a time, it is more convenient to have them in the same group window.

The customized group window that is created in this chapter is called Desktop. You can give it another name if you prefer.

# OPENING WINDOWS

When you boot up your computer, your opening screen will appear blank except for the DOS (C:\>) prompt. If you are tired of looking at the Windows logo when you boot up Windows, try the startup command below:

```
C:\> win :
```

1. **Type win :** (there's a space between win and the colon) at the C:\> (DOS prompt) and **press Enter**. The hourglass icon will appear and the logo will not. After a brief period, the Program Manager opening screen will appear.

# OPENING A NEW GROUP

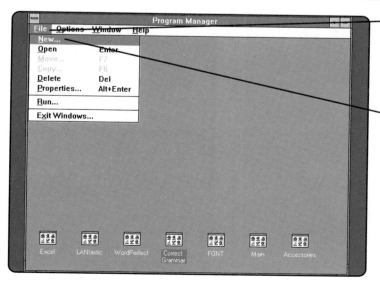

1. **Click** on **File** in the Program Manager menu bar. A pull-down menu will appear.

2. **Click** on **New**. The New Program Object dialog box will appear.

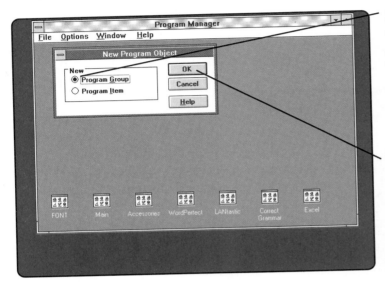

3. **Click** on the **Program Group circle** (called an *option button*) to place a black dot inside the circle. If there is already a black dot inside the circle, go on to step 4.

4. **Click** on **OK**. The Program Group Properties dialog box will appear.

Notice that the cursor will be blinking in the Description text box until you begin typing.

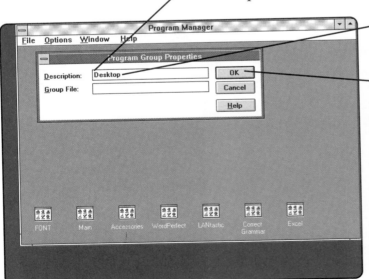

5. **Type Desktop** in the Description text box.

6. **Click** on **OK**. An hourglass will appear briefly and then the new group window called Desktop will appear.

7. Decide what programs you want to place on your desktop and follow the steps below. (You may or may not select the same programs we use in our examples.)

# PLACING PROGRAM ICONS

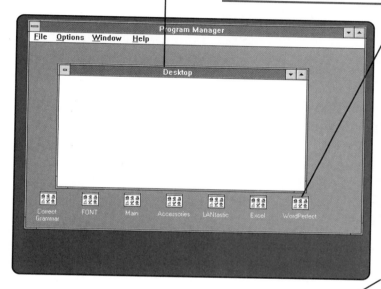

1. **Click twice** on the **group icon** containing the program you want to move to the Desktop group window. In this example it is the WordPerfect group icon. The WordPerfect group window will appear. If your Desktop group window blocks your view, move it. See Chapter 2, "Changing the Size and Position of a Window."

2. **Move** the mouse arrow to the **program icon** you selected (in this example, the WordPerfect icon).

3. **Press and hold** the left mouse button as you **drag** the **program icon** to the Desktop group window.

4. **Release** the left mouse button. The Desktop group window will move to the foreground. The program icon will appear on it. The other group window will move to the background. If you want to return to the other group window just click anywhere on it.

# COMPLETING YOUR CUSTOMIZED GROUP WINDOW

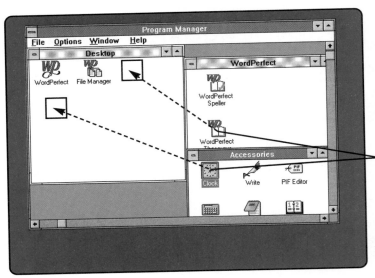

You can now place the program icons of the Windows or DOS applications that you use most often into your customized group windows.

To move each program icon to your customized group window, repeat steps 1 to 4 in the previous section entitled, "Placing Program Icons."

The organizational possibilities are endless. There are no rules about where you should place program icons within a window or into which group window. It really gets down to how you think you can work best. Productivity is the name of the game in Windows. You are limited only by your own imagination!

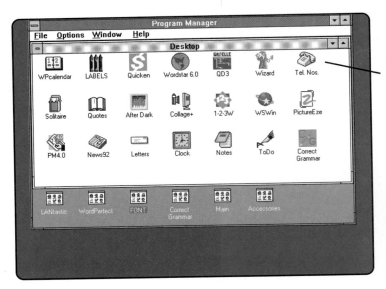

This is an illustration of a completely customized group window. The program icons are organized so that the icons in the top row represent software applications designed for DOS. The program icons in the bottom two rows represent software applications designed for Windows.

# CLOSING A GROUP WINDOW

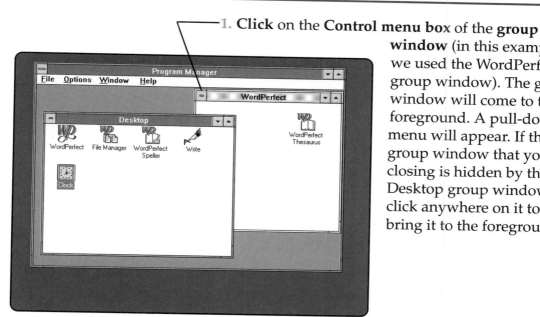

1. **Click** on the **Control menu box** of the **group window** (in this example we used the WordPerfect group window). The group window will come to the foreground. A pull-down menu will appear. If the group window that you are closing is hidden by the Desktop group window, click anywhere on it to bring it to the foreground.

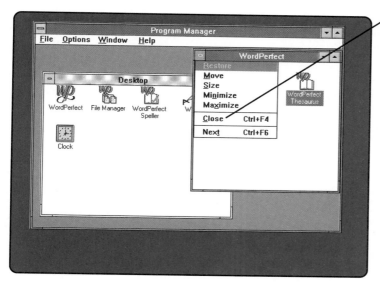

2. **Click** on **Close**. The group window will disappear. The group icon of the window you closed (e.g. WordPerfect) will appear at the bottom of the Program Manager window beside the other group icons.

In Chapter 6 you will set up DOS programs to work in Windows. You will also move them to and arrange them on your customized Desktop group window.

# Setting Up Your DOS Programs for Windows

Most DOS applications are set up by the 3.1 installation program automatically. Since some DOS programs cannot be set up by the 3.1 installation program, you may want to add a DOS program yourself. Windows offers three methods to make a program icon for a DOS program so that it can be used in Windows.

In this chapter you will make an icon for DOS programs using three methods:

❖ The Search for Applications method

❖ The Specify an Application method

❖ The PIF Editor method

## ADVANTAGES OF THE THREE SETUP METHODS

Method #1, on page 55, the Search for Applications method, searches your hard disk drive for applications to set up automatically. Use this method when you want to set up many different program icons at once.

**Method #1: Search for Applications method**

Windows Setup    A DOS Program Icon

Setup Applications

Setup can either search for applications to set up for use with Windows, or ask you to specify an application to set up.

Setup will:

◉ Search for applications.

○ Ask you to specify an application.

| OK | Cancel | Help |

The Search for Applications method will take longer than the Specify an Application method if you only want to set up one DOS program. Also, it automatically places all the newly created program icons in an Applications group window rather than in the group window of your choice.

**51**

Method #2, on page 63, the Specify an Application method, sets up one program icon at a time. This method is faster than the Search for Applications method because it allows you to specify in advance:

❖ The group window in which you want the newlycreated program icon to be placed automatically. For example, you can specify that you want the newly created program icon to be located in your customized Desktop group window.

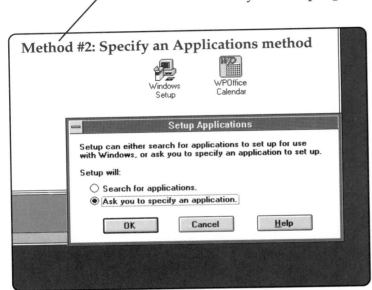

Method #2: Specify an Applications method

To use this method, it is helpful if you are somewhat familiar with the language of DOS and know the location of the program you are setting up. In this method you will write a DOS path statement that tells Windows the name of your *execution file* (the file that makes the program run) and the *directory* (location) where the file is stored. How the path statement works is explained on page 65 in the section entitled "Method #2: Specify an Application."

Method #3, on page 67, the PIF Editor method, uses the Windows PIF (Program Information File) Editor to set up programs to work in Windows. Some DOS programs do not lend themselves to being set up by Methods #1 and #2. In that case, use this method.

In this method you will write a DOS path statement that tells Windows the name of your execution file (the file that makes the program run) and the directory (location) where the file is stored. How the path works is explained later in the section entitled "Method #2: Specify an Application," on page 65.

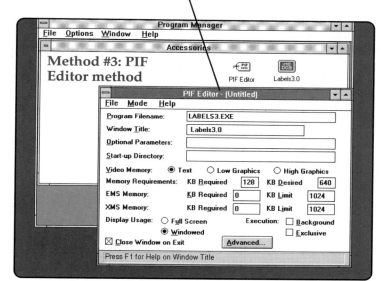

In addition, Method #3 uses a two-step process to complete the task. The PIF Editor does not automatically produce an icon for the DOS program when it sets it up to work in Windows. Therefore, Method #3 requires you to use the Program Item Properties dialog box to make a program icon after the PIF Editor has done its work.

# OPENING THE WINDOWS SETUP DIALOG BOX

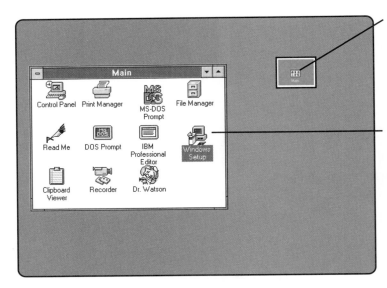

1. **Click twice** on the **Main group icon**, which is located at the bottom of your screen. The Main group window will appear.

2. **Click twice** on the **Windows Setup icon**. The Windows Setup dialog box will appear.

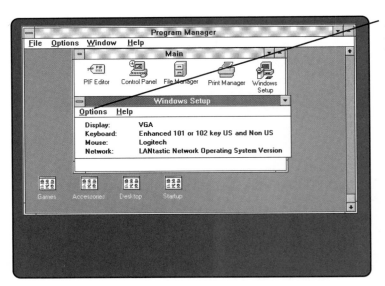

3. **Click** on **Options**. A pull-down menu will appear.

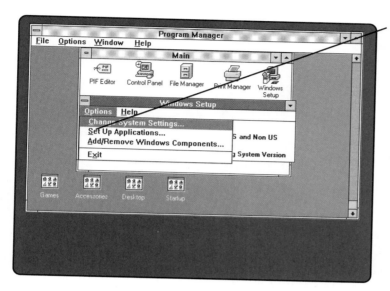

**4. Click** on **Set Up Applications**. The Setup Applications dialog box will appear. You are now ready to begin either Method #1, below, or Method #2 later in this chapter.

# METHOD #1: SEARCH FOR APPLICATIONS

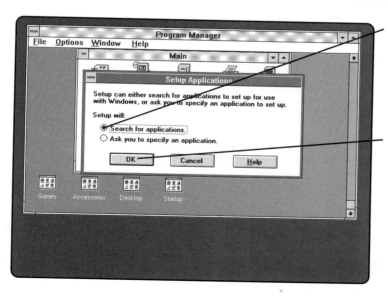

**1. Click** on **Search for applications** to place a black dot in the circle. If the circle already has a dot in the center, go on to step 2.

**2. Click** on **OK**. The next Setup Applications dialog box will appear.

3. **Click** on **C: (Local Drive)** in the list box.

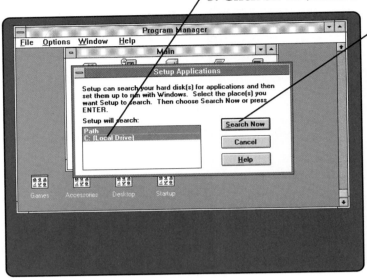

4. **Click** on **Search Now**. The Windows Setup program will begin searching the drive for programs that it can automatically set up for use in Windows. When Windows Setup finds an application but is uncertain of its name, it will pause and another Setup Applications dialog box will appear like the one below. Depending on how many programs you have on your hard drive, the sequence below (steps 5 and 6) may be repeated more than once until the search is complete.

5. **Click** on the **correct name** for the program. In this example, the correct name is Quicken (this is the DOS version). The program listed in your Setup Applications dialog box may be different. (Or, if the program is already set up, or you don't want to set it up, or you don't know the correct name, click on Cancel.) If you click on Cancel, the search will continue to the next DOS application.

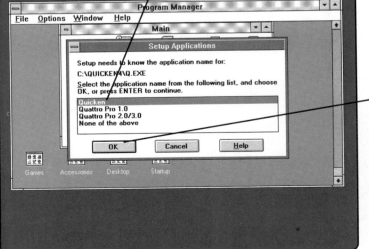

6. **Click** on **OK**. The search will continue. When the search is complete another Setup Applications dialog box will appear like the one on the next page. This dialog box contains a list of the applications Setup found in its search.

# SELECTING DOS PROGRAMS TO SET UP FOR WINDOWS

1. **Move** the mouse arrow to the **scroll box**.

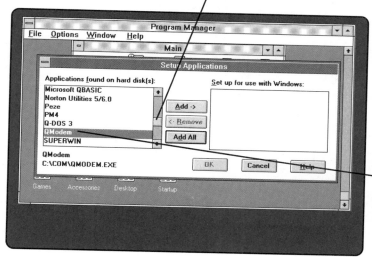

2. **Press** and **hold** the left mouse button as you move the **scroll box** up or down to search the list of programs that Windows is ready to set up. **Release** the mouse button when you have found the program you want.

3. **Click** on the **DOS application** that you want to set up. It will become highlighted (in this example, QModem is highlighted).

4. **Click** on **Add** on the screen above. QModem will move from the "Applications found on hard disk(s):" box on the left to the "Set up for use with Windows:" box on the right. **Repeat steps 1 to 3** until the list of DOS applications you want to set up is complete.

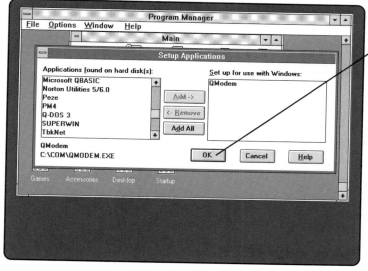

5. **Click** on **OK**. The Windows Setup dialog box will appear. The application(s) that you selected will be set up automatically. Their program icons are now located in a new Applications group icon, which you will find at the bottom of the Program Manager screen.

# CLOSING WINDOWS SETUP

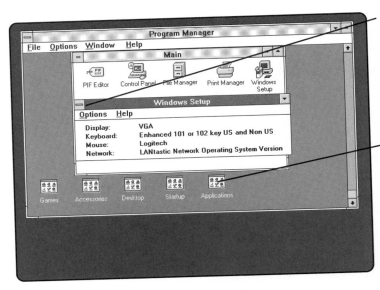

1. **Click** on the **Control menu box** on the left corner of the Windows Setup dialog box title bar. A pull-down menu will appear.

Notice the Applications group icon that was created automatically in the previous section of this chapter.

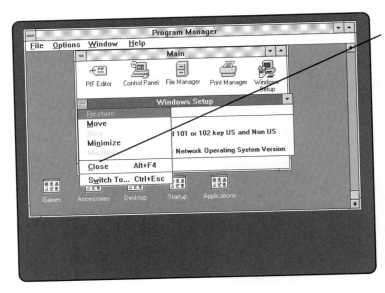

2. **Click** on **Close**. The Windows Setup dialog box will disappear and the Main group window will now be in the foreground.

**3. Click** on the **Control menu box** on the left of the Main group window title bar. A pull-down menu will appear.

**4. Click** on **Close**. The Main group window will disappear. The Program Manager screen will appear.

**5. Click twice** on the **Applications group icon** at the bottom of your Program Manager screen. The Applications group window will appear. It will contain the icon of the DOS program you created. In this example, the program icon is for QMODEM.

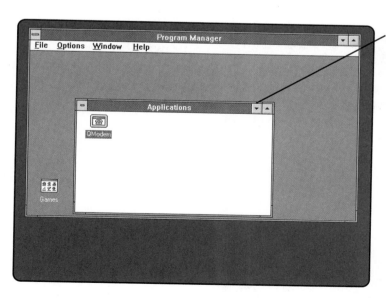

**6. Click** on the **Minimize button (▼)** on the right of the Applications group window title bar. The Applications group window will disappear. The Applications group icon will appear at the bottom of your Program Manager screen.

# MOVING A DOS PROGRAM ICON TO YOUR CUSTOMIZED GROUP WINDOW

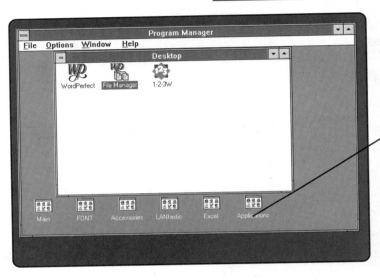

1. **Open** your **Desktop group window** if you have not already done so by **clicking twice** on the **Desktop group icon** at the bottom of your screen.

2. **Click twice** on the **Applications group icon** that you created with Windows Setup in the previous sections. The Applications group window will appear and will overlay the Desktop group window.

3. **Move** the mouse arrow to the **program icon**.

4. **Press** and **hold** the left mouse button as you **drag** the **program icon** up to the dimmed Desktop group window title bar. If you can't find it, you may have to move the Applications group window. See "Changing the Position of a Window" in Chapter 2.

5. **Release** the mouse button. The Applications group window will move to the background. The Desktop group window will move to the foreground. The program icon will appear on the Desktop group window. If you created other program icons, move them now.

# DELETING A GROUP ICON

Now that you have moved the DOS icons to the Desktop group window, it is a good idea to delete the empty Applications group since it no longer serves a useful purpose.

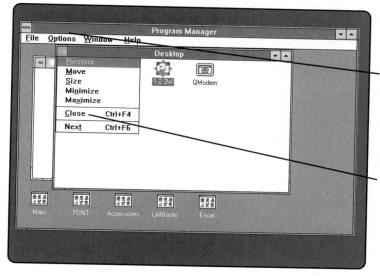

1. **Click** on the **Control menu box** in the left corner of the Desktop group window title bar. A pull-down menu will appear.

2. **Click** on **Close**. The Desktop group window will disappear. The empty Applications group window will come to the foreground. The Desktop group icon will appear at the bottom of your screen.

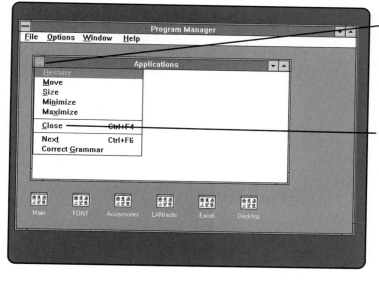

3. **Click** on the **Control menu box** on the left of the Applications group window title bar. A pull-down menu will appear.

4. **Click** on **Close**. The Applications group window will disappear and the Applications group icon will appear at the bottom of your screen.

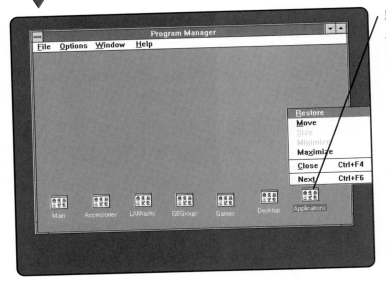

5. **Click once** on the **Applications group icon**. (Make certain you do not click twice.) The Applications group icon title will become highlighted and a pop-up menu will appear. Ignore the pop-up menu and go on to step 6.

6. **Click** on **File** in the Program Manager menu bar. A pull-down menu will appear and the pop-up menu will disappear.

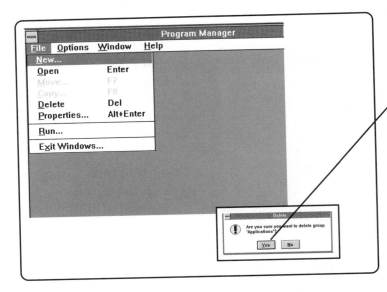

7. **Click** on **Delete**. The pull-down menu will disappear. The Delete dialog box will appear.

8. **Click** on **Yes**. The Delete dialog box will disappear, the Applications group will be deleted and you will be returned to the Program Manager or your Desktop group window.

# METHOD #2:
# SPECIFY AN APPLICATION

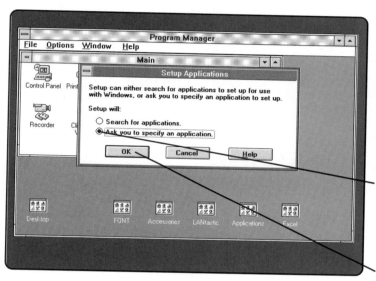

1. **Open** the **Setup Applications dialog box**. If you need help opening the Setup Applications dialog box, see steps 1 to 4 in "Opening the Windows Setup" at the beginning of this chapter.

2. **Click** on **Ask you to specify an application** to place a black dot in the circle.

3. **Click** on **OK**. Another Setup Applications dialog box will appear.

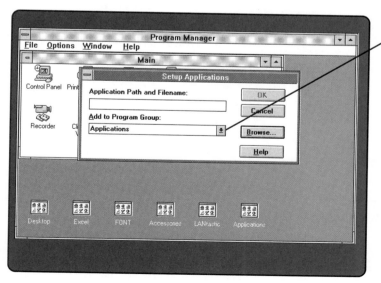

4. **Click** on the **down arrow** on the Add to Program Group list box. A pull-down list of available groups will appear. **Continue clicking** on the **down arrow** until Desktop appears.

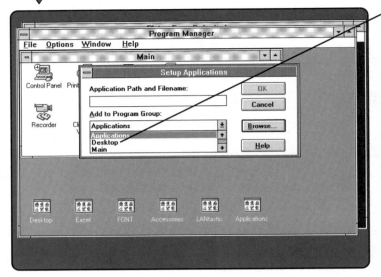

5. **Click** on **Desktop**. It will become highlighted. The pull-down list of available groups will disappear. By selecting the Desktop group from the list, you have specified in advance to Windows where you want to locate the DOS program icon you are about to make.

6. **Click** on the **Application Path** and **Filename text box**. A blinking cursor will appear in the text box.

7. **Type** the **path** of the DOS program you want to set up for use in Windows. The path is the location of the file. If you are not familiar with the term path see the explanation on the next page *before* going to step 8.

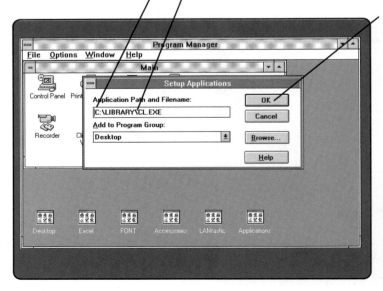

8. **Click** on **OK**. Another Setup Applications dialog box may appear depending on the DOS application you have chosen. (If the program icon already exists, a dialog box will appear and ask you to replace it or create an additional program icon.) If the Setup Applications dialog box does not appear, the Windows Setup dialog box will appear instead. In that case, go on to step 11.

The DOS *path statement* for any file is a description of its location on your hard disk drive. The best way to understand path is to think of it as the directions you might give someone to get to your house. For example, the disk drive might be thought of as the state where the file lives, the directory as the town, and the filename as the street address. The path normally includes the following elements:

❶ The name of the hard disk drive. For most computers this would be drive C:

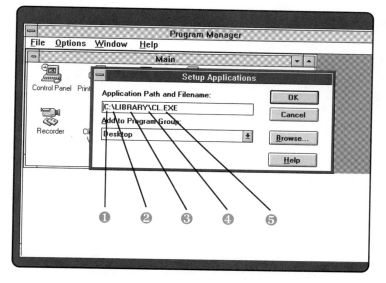

❷ A backslash (\). The backslash is used to separate the drive name, the directory name, and the filename in the path description

❸ The name of the directory where the program is located (in this case, LIBRARY)

❹ Another backslash(\).

❺ The name of the file. The name of the file also includes its extension, which is the letters or numbers after the period (.) in its name. In this example, the name of the file that runs our WordPerfect calendar is CL.EXE.

The name of the file that makes a DOS program run usually has an extension that ends in .EXE. However, some programs use other extensions such as .BAT.

If you do not know the name of the file which will run your DOS program or its path, refer to the user's manual that came with your software program.

9. **Click** on the **name** of the DOS application. In this example, the correct name is WPOffice Calendar. If you typed the name of a different program in your path statement in step 7, its name will appear here.

10. **Click** on **OK**. The Setup Applications dialog box will disappear and the Windows Setup menu will reappear. A program icon for the DOS program you specified to be set up is now located in the customized Desktop group.

11. **Click** on the **Control menu box** on the left corner of the Windows Setup menu title bar. A pull-down menu will appear.

12. **Click** on **Close**. The Windows Setup menu will disappear.

13. **Click** on the **Control menu box** on the left of the Main group window title bar. A pull-down menu will appear.

14. **Click** on **Close**. The Main group window will disappear and the Main group icon will appear at the bottom of your screen.

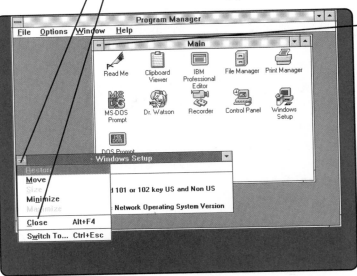

# METHOD #3: THE PIF EDITOR

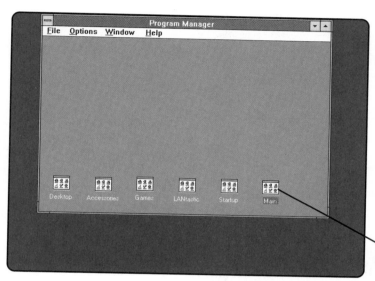

There are some DOS programs that the Windows Setup program (Methods #1 and #2) cannot set up. If you find that you cannot set up a program with the first two methods described earlier in this chapter, then the PIF Editor method probably will work.

**1. Click twice** on the **Main group icon**. The Main group window will appear. (Your screen may be different depending on whether or not you have left your Desktop group window or some other group window open).

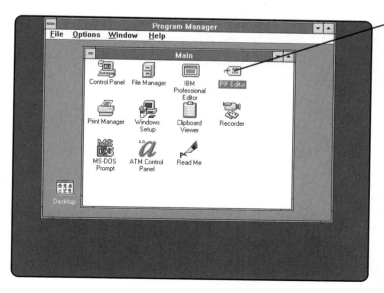

**2. Click twice** on the **PIF Editor program icon**. The PIF Editor dialog box will appear.

3. **Type** the **name** of the DOS program execution file that you want to set up in the Program Filename text box. In this example, the DOS program execution file is LABELS.EXE. If you do not know the name of the file that makes your DOS program run, refer to your software user's manual.

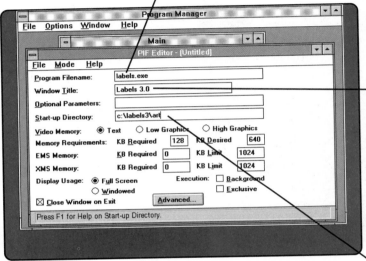

4. **Press** the **Tab** key. The cursor will move to the Window Title text box.

5. **Type** the **name** of the DOS program in the Window Title text box. In this example, the program's name is LABELS3.0.

6. **Press** the **Tab** key **twice**. The cursor will move to the Start-up Directory text box.

7. **Type** the **name** of the directory where the program execution file is located in the Start-up Directory text box. If you do not know the name of the directory where the program file is located, refer to the installation section of your software user's manual. If you can't find it there, a telephone call to the software's technical service will do the trick.

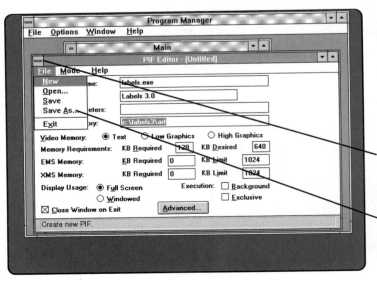

8. **Click** on **File** in the PIF Editor menu bar. A pull-down menu will appear.

9. **Click** on **Save As**. The Save As dialog box will appear.

10. **Click** on the **File Name text box** and **drag** the **cursor** to highlight **\*.pif**. Then **type** a **name** for the new PIF file of eight or fewer letters. Add a .PIF extension to the filename.

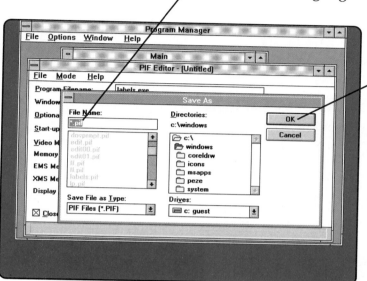

11. **Click** on **OK**. The Save As dialog box will disappear. The PIF Editor dialog box will move to the foreground. Before you can use this program in Windows, you must assign a program icon to it. To do this you must first close the PIF Editor and return to your Desktop group window.

12. **Click** on the **Control menu box** on the left of the PIF Editor dialog box title bar. A pull-down menu will appear.

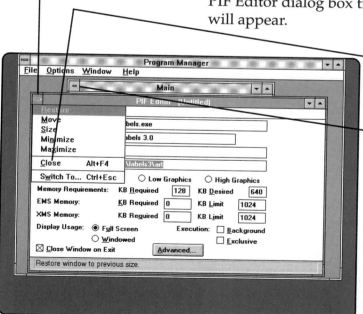

13. **Click on Close**. The PIF Editor dialog box will disappear.

14. **Click twice** on the **Control menu box** on the left of the Main group window title bar. The Main group window will disappear. The Program Manager screen will appear. If you have left your Desktop group window open it will move to the foreground.

# MAKING AN ICON FOR A PIF FILE

Method #3, the PIF Editor, does not automatically create an icon for the new PIF file when you save it. To run your DOS application after you made the PIF file, you must create the icon.

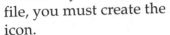

**1. Open** your **Desktop group window** if you have not already done so.

**2. Click** on **File** in the Program Manager menu bar. A pull-down menu will appear.

**3. Click** on **New**. The New Program Object dialog box will appear.

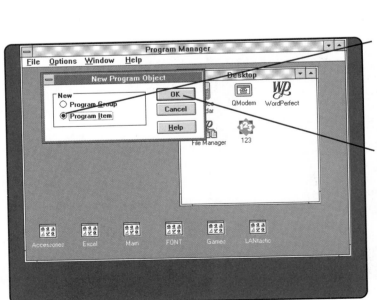

**4. Click** on **Program Item** to place a black dot in the center of each circle. (If the circle already has a black dot, go on to step 5).

**5. Click** on **OK**. The Program Item Properties dialog box will appear.

6. **Type** the **name** of the DOS program in the Description text box.

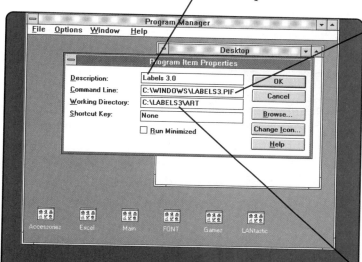

7. **Type** the **path** of the DOS program's PIF file that you just created on the Command Line text box. The path of a newly created PIF file should always include the WINDOWS directory. If you need more information about the path, see the section entitled "Method #2: Specify an Application" in this chapter.

8. **Type** the **path** of the directory where the DOS program is located.

9. **Click** on **OK**. The Program Item Properties dialog box will disappear. The icon for the DOS program will appear on your Desktop group window.

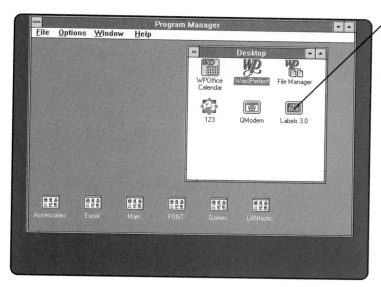

In this example, the Labels 3.0 icon represents the DOS program set up by the PIF Editor in the previous section, on pages 67 to 69.

# ARRANGING YOUR WORK AREA

If you intend to add other program icons to your customized group window, it is a good idea to size the window so that it fills the work area. You may also want to place your program icons in specific locations.

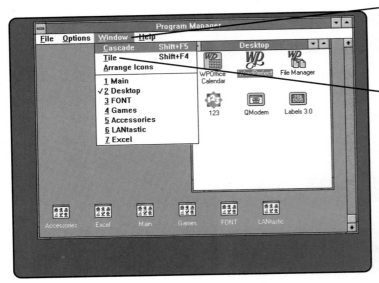

1. **Click** on **Options** in the Program Manager menu bar. A pull-down menu will appear.

2. **Click** on **Auto Arrange**. If there is a check mark on Auto Arrange, click anywhere on the desktop. The menu will disappear. Clicking on Auto Arrange tells Windows to place the group icons at the bottom of your screen and the program icons in the Desktop group window into neat rows.

3. **Click** on **Window** in the Program Manager menu bar. A pull-down menu will appear.

4. **Click** on **Tile**. The Desktop group window will expand to fill the standard window size. The group icons will line up neatly at the bottom of the screen. The program icons on the Desktop group window will line up in horizontal rows.

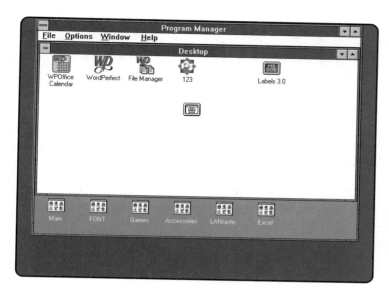

5. **Move** the mouse arrow to a **program icon** that you want to move.

6. **Press and hold** the left mouse button as you **drag** the **program icon** to a new location on the Desktop group window.

7. **Release** the left mouse button. The program icon will be lined up in its new location.

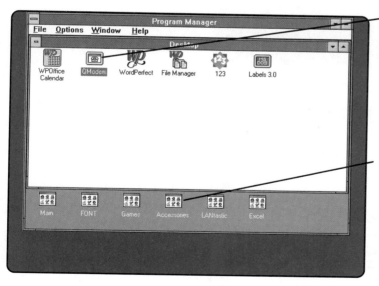

Notice that the QModem icon is now located here.

If there are other program icons whose position on your Desktop group window you would like to change, repeat steps 5 to 7.

If you want to take icons from other group windows and add them to the Desktop group window, see the section entitled "Placing Program Icons" in Chapter 5.

# SAVING THE CUSTOMIZED DESKTOP GROUP WINDOW

Once you have set up your customized Desktop group window, the next step is to save it so that each time you start Windows it will be the first window you see.

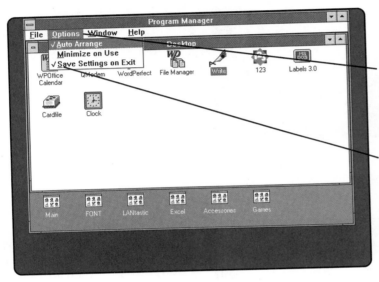

1. **Click** on **Options** in the Program Manager menu bar. A pull-down menu will appear.

2. **Click** on **Save Settings on Exit**. If the Save Settings on Exit option is already checked, click anywhere on your desktop. The pull-down menu will disappear.

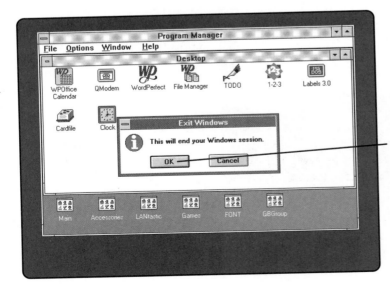

3. **Press and hold** the **Alt** key and **press** the **F4** key (Alt + F4). The Exit Windows dialog box will appear.

4. **Click** on **OK**. You will be returned to DOS.

5. **Type win** at the DOS prompt (C:\>) and **press Enter**. Your screen will go blank for a moment. The Windows opening screen will appear briefly. Then the hourglass will appear briefly and Windows will start up. The first thing you will see is your Desktop group window. It will look exactly like it did when you exited Windows.

6. **Click** on **Options** in the Program Manager menu bar. A pull-down menu will appear.

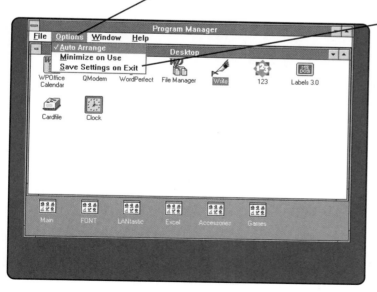

7. **Click** on **Save Settings on Exit**. The pull-down menu will disappear. When next you exit and restart Windows, the Desktop group window screen settings will be the way you last saved it.

# Customizing Startups

This chapter will show you how to organize your working files (document files) so that you can be more efficient. In this chapter you will:

❖ Make a working directory

❖ Write a path statement to boot a program to a working directory

❖ Write a command statement to boot to a specific file

❖ Set up Windows so that important programs are automatically booted up when you boot up Windows

## ADVANTAGES OF A WORKING DIRECTORY

Normally when you save a file, it is sent to the main program's directory (in this example, the WINDOWS directory). This is inefficient for several reasons:

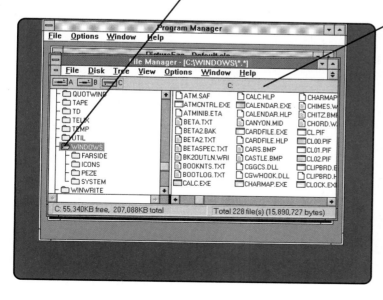

❖ When all kinds of files are stored together in one directory, as in the example you see here, it's difficult to find a specific file among a long list of document files. This is especially true when you are searching for a word processing document.

❖ It is time-consuming to scroll down a long list of files to search for the file you want to open.

**77**

In contrast to keeping files in a large program directory, the advantages of putting your document files in a smaller working directory are:

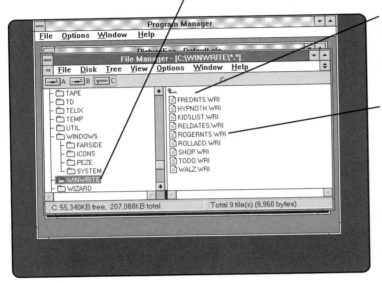

❖ It is easy to find a file when it is contained in a short list of related files in a working directory.

❖ It is easier to back up a group of working files if they are all in a directory where there are no other types of files.

# MAKING A WORKING DIRECTORY

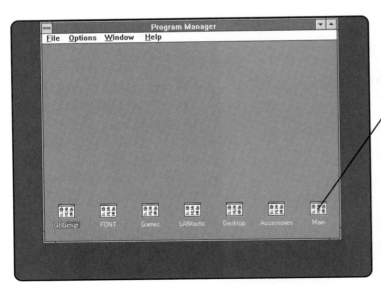

1. **Click twice** on the **Main group icon**. The Main group window will appear.

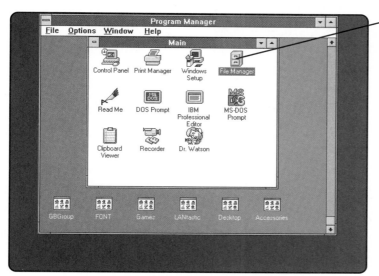

**2. Click twice** on the **File Manager icon**. The File Manager window will appear.

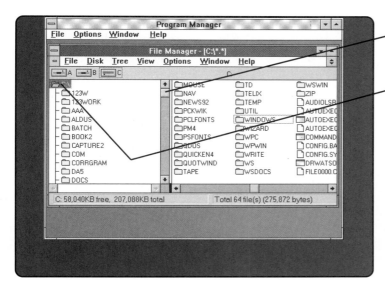

**3. Scroll** to the **top** of the **directory list**.

**4. Click** on the **C:\ directory icon**. It will be highlighted. This is the root or main directory of your hard disk drive. The files and directories contained in the root directory will be listed in the list box on the right.

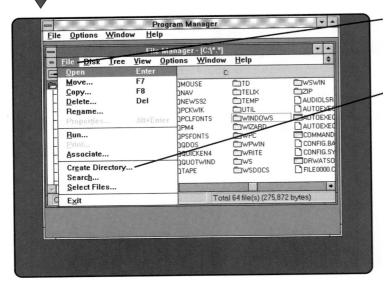

5. **Click** on **File** in the File Manager menu bar. A pull-down menu will appear.

6. **Click** on **Create Directory**. The Create Directory dialog box will appear.

Notice that the cursor is flashing in the Name text box.

7. **Type** the **name** of your new working directory (in this example, **WINWRITE**) in the Name text box.

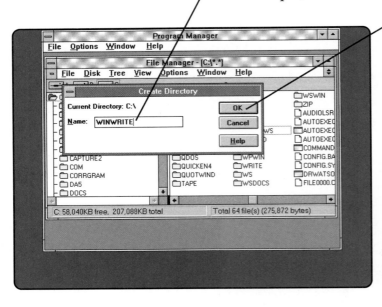

8. **Click** on **OK**. The Create Directory dialog box will disappear. The File Manager dialog box will come to the foreground. The name of the working directory that you just typed (WINWRITE) will appear, listed alphabetically, in the C: list box on the right. This list box contains a list of all of the files and directories stored in the main or root directory.

9. **Click twice** on the **name** of the new working directory (in this example, **WINWRITE**).

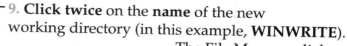

The File Manager dialog box will now show the WINWRITE working directory in the list box on the left (see below).

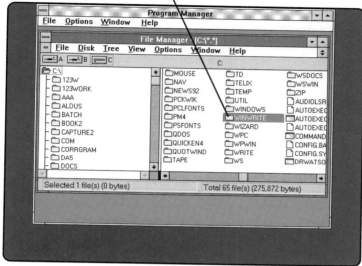

This list box contains a list of all the directories on your hard disk drive.

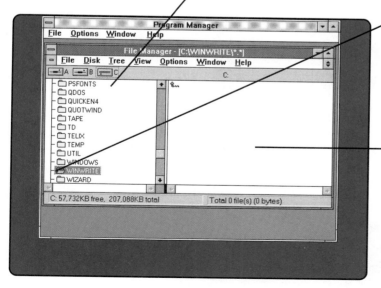

When you click on a directory name in the list box on the left to highlight it, a list of the files stored in that directory appears in the list box on the right.

Notice that the WINWRITE directory contains no files at this time since you have not saved or moved any files to this directory. See the section in Chapter 18 entitled "Moving Files with Drag and Drop" if you want to move files now.

# CLOSING FILE MANAGER

1. **Click** on the **Control menu box** on the left of the File Manager title bar. A pull-down menu will appear.

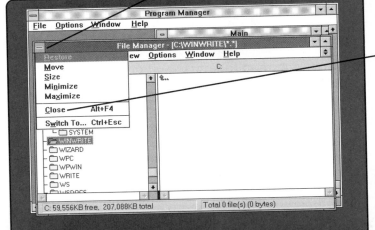

2. **Click** on **Close**. The File Manager window will disappear. The Main group window will appear.

3. **Click** on the **Control menu box** on the left of the Main group window title bar. A pull-down menu will appear.

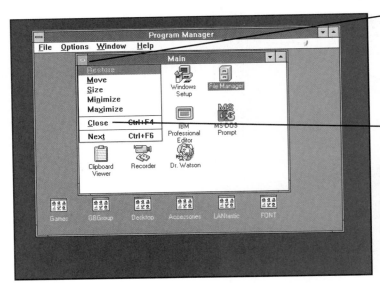

4. **Click** on **Close**. The Main group window will disappear and the Main group icon will appear at the bottom of the Program Manager screen.

# BOOTING TO A
# WORKING DIRECTORY

Windows, like many software programs, automatically stores document files in a *default directory*. (A default directory usually is the place where most of the operating files are located.) In this example, the WINDOWS directory is the default directory for the Windows Write program. You can set up any Windows-based program so that it will place its document files in a specific working directory that you create.

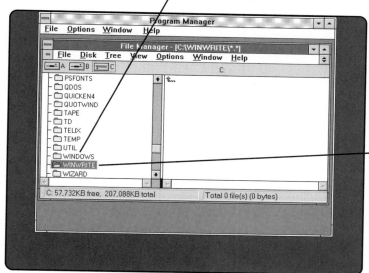

In this example, you will write a path statement that will tell Windows to store your Windows Write document files in the WINWRITE working directory you created in the previous section.

1. **Open** your customized **Desktop group window** if it contains the Windows Write program icon. If you did not move the Write icon to your Desktop group window earlier, then open the Accessories group window. If you need help opening a group window, see the section entitled "Opening a Group Window" in Chapter 1.

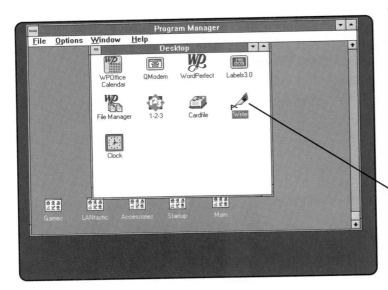

2. **Click once** on the **Write icon** (be careful not to click twice). The icon will become highlighted.

3. **Click** on **File** in the Program Manager menu bar. A pull-down menu will appear.

4. **Click** on **Properties**. The Program Item Properties dialog box will appear.

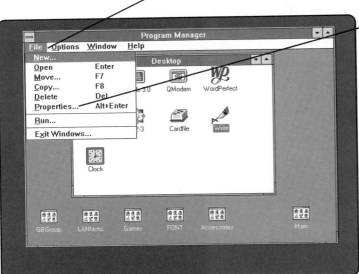

5. **Move** mouse arrow to the **Working Directory text box**. **Click** to set the cursor for typing.

6. **Type** the **path** of the working directory (in this case, **C:\WINWRITE**) where you want Windows Write to store your document files. If you need help understanding the path, see Chapter 6, the section entitled "Method #2: Specify an Application."

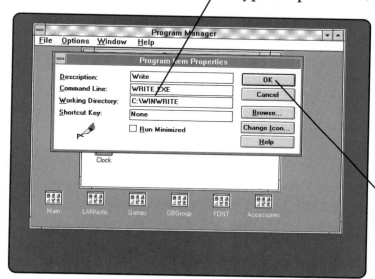

7. **Click** on **OK**. The Desktop group window will appear (or the group window where your Windows Write program is located.)

8. **Click twice** on the **Write icon**. The opening screen (Page 1) of an untitled Windows Write document file will appear.

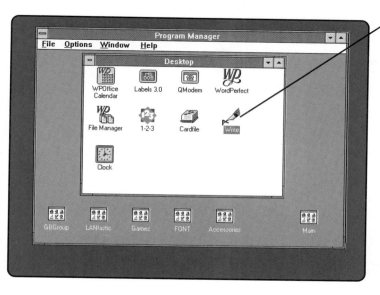

9. **Click** on **File** in the Windows Write menu bar. A pull-down menu will appear.

10. **Click** on **Open**. The Open dialog box will appear.

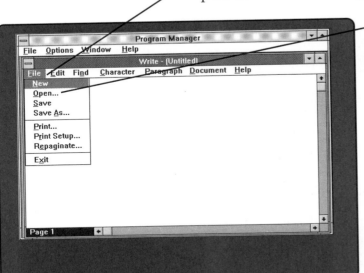

The Open dialog box displays a list of the files in the WINWRITE working directory. Since you just created it, your WINWRITE working directory will not contain document files at this time. This list of WRI files is an example of what your directory will look like once you have saved or moved files into it. In the next section you will create a document file and save it to the WINWRITE directory.

Notice that Windows Write document files have the extension .WRI.

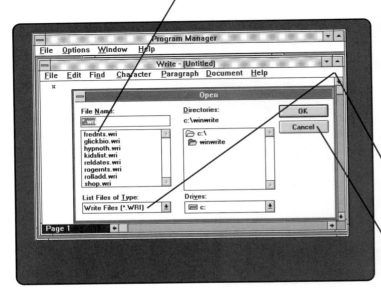

11. **Click** on **Cancel**. The Write (Untitled) screen will reappear.

# CREATING AND SAVING A WINDOWS WRITE DOCUMENT

In this section you will create and then save a Windows Write document file to the WINWRITE working directory you created in the last section. In the section entitled "Booting to a Specific File," you will set up the Windows Write icon to boot up (open)

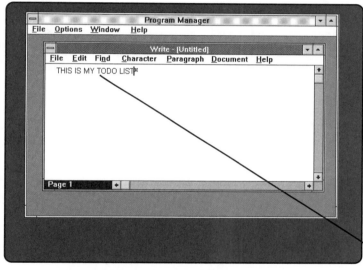

directly to that document file in the WINWRITE working directory. The advantages of setting up an icon to open a document file directly are that Windows will have a faster opening time and you will have to perform fewer "mouse clicks." To do this you will create a Windows Write document file entitled TODO and save it.

**1. Type THIS IS MY TODO LIST**.

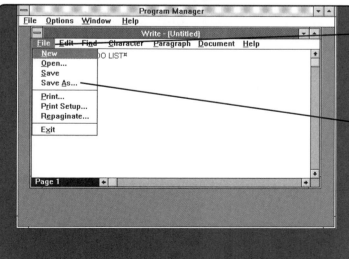

**2. Click** on **File** in the Windows Write menu bar. A pull-down menu will appear.

**3. Click** on **Save As**. The Save As dialog box will appear.

4. **Move** the mouse arrow to the **File Name text box**.

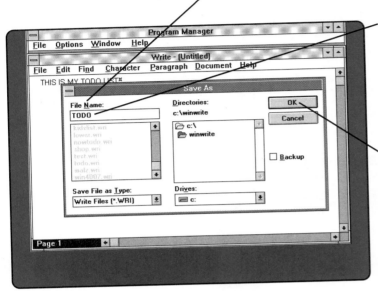

5. **Type** the filename **TODO**. (You are naming the file "TODO" instead of "TO DO" because Windows does not accept spaces in filenames.)

6. **Click** on **OK**. The Save As dialog box will disappear. The Windows Write opening screen (Page 1) will appear.

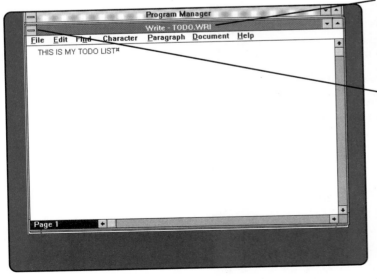

Notice that the document's name in the title bar has changed from "Untitled" to "TODO.WRI."

7. **Click twice** on the **Control menu box** on the left corner of the Windows Write title bar. This will close the Windows Write program. The Desktop group window will appear (or the Accessories group window if that is where your Write program icon is located). Congratulations! You have now created a Windows Write document file called TODO.WRI and saved it to the WINWRITE working directory that you created earlier.

# BOOTING TO A SPECIFIC FILE

In this section, you will set up the Windows Write program so that it will open the TODO.WRI file automatically when you click twice on the Windows Write program icon. The TODO.WRI file is the document file that you created in the last section.

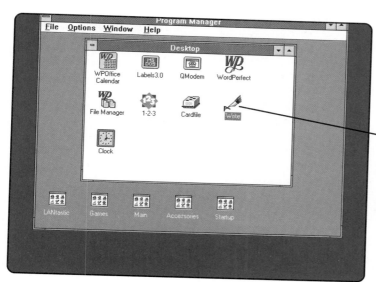

1. **Click once** on the Windows **Write program icon** to highlight it. Be certain to click only once or you will boot up the program instead of highlighting the icon. If the icon is already highlighted, go on to step 2.

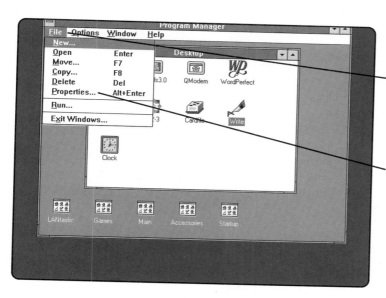

2. **Click** on **File** in the Program Manager menu bar. A pull-down menu will appear.

3. **Click** on **Properties**. The Program Item Properties dialog box will appear.

Notice that the Program Item Properties dialog box for Windows Write shows that the program is set up to store its files in the working directory called WINWRITE that you created earlier in this chapter.

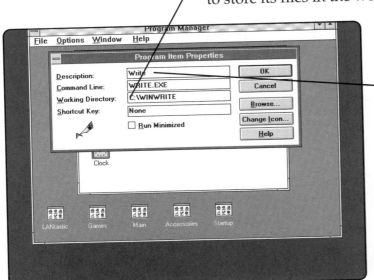

**4. Move** the mouse arrow to the **Description text box** and **click** to set the cursor at the beginning of the word "Write."

**5. Press and hold** the left mouse button as you **drag** the **cursor** across the word "Write." It will become highlighted. **Release** the mouse button.

6. **Type To Do** in the **Description text box**.

7. **Move** mouse arrow to the **Command Line text box** and **click** to set the cursor at the end of "WRITE.EXE."

**8. Press** the **space bar** to move one space to the right.

9. **Type TODO.WRI**.

10. **Click** on **OK**. The Program Item Properties dialog box will disappear. The Desktop group window will come to the foreground.

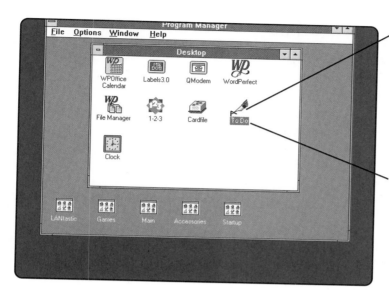

**11. Click twice** on the Windows **Write program icon**. The opening screen (Page 1) of the TODO.WRI document file you created earlier in this chapter will appear.

Notice that the Write program icon is now labeled "To Do."

Congratulations! You have just mastered one of the many ways Windows allows you to work more efficiently. As you can see, setting up a program icon to boot up directly to a specific file is faster than opening the program first and then opening the file. You can use this method to open automatically any document file with any program icon.

**12. Close** the **TODO.WRI** file. If you need help closing the file, see the section in this chapter entitled "Creating and Saving a Windows Write Document."

# AUTOMATING YOUR STARTUPS

Windows has a wonderful feature called Startup. It makes it possible for you to boot up specific programs automatically when you boot up Windows. Not only does this feature speed up the time it takes to boot up the programs you plan to work on but also it saves a lot of mouse clicks! In this section you will:

❖ Move the Write To Do icon and the Clock icon from your customized Desktop group window to the Startup group window

❖ Set both icons so they will be minimized when started

❖ Set up Windows so it will save your new settings when you exit

❖ Exit Windows and then reboot Windows with the Startup feature automatically booting up your Clock and your To Do Write program as minimized icons

1. **Open** your **Desktop group window** (or the Accessories group window that contains your Write To Do icon that you created in the previous section). If you need help opening your Desktop group window, see Chapter 1, the section entitled "Opening a Group Window."

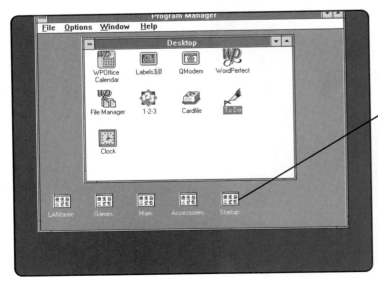

2. **Click twice** on the **Startup group icon** at the bottom of your screen. (Your screen may look different from this one.) The Startup group window will appear. The Desktop group window will recede into the background.

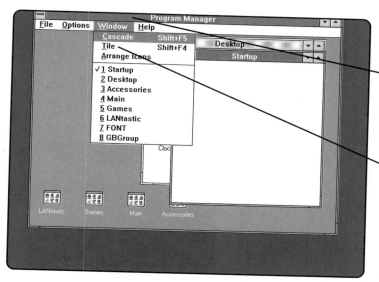

3. **Click** on **Window** in the Program Manager menu bar. A pull-down menu will appear.

4. **Click** on **Tile**. The two group windows will now be placed side by side.

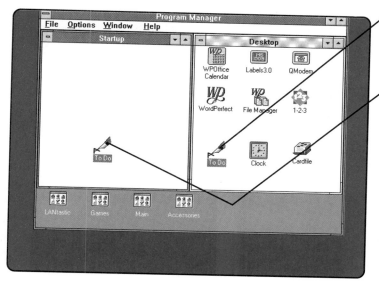

5. **Move** the mouse arrow to the Windows **Write To Do icon**.

6. **Press and hold** the left mouse button as you **drag** it to the Startup group window. **Release** the mouse button when the icon is placed where you want it to be located.

7. **Repeat steps 5 and 6** to move the Clock icon to the Startup group window.

**8. Click once** on the Windows **Write To Do icon** to highlight it. Be certain to click only once or you will boot up the program.

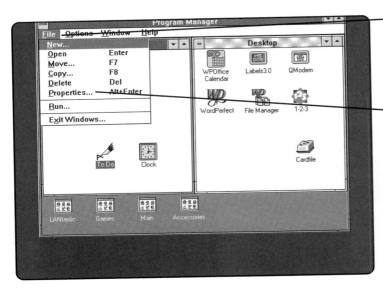

**9. Click** on **File** in the Program Manager menu bar. A pull-down menu will appear.

**10. Click** on **Properties**. The Program Item Properties dialog box will appear.

**11. Click** on **Run Minimized** to put an X in the check box. If there is already an X in the box, click on Cancel and go to step 13.

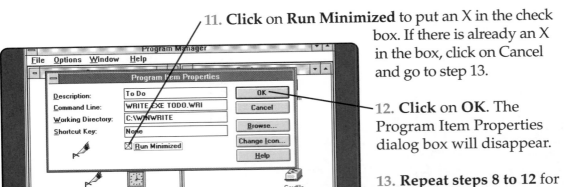

**12. Click** on **OK**. The Program Item Properties dialog box will disappear.

**13. Repeat steps 8 to 12** for the Clock icon.

**14. Click twice** on the **Write To Do icon**. It will be minimized at the bottom of your screen.

**15. Click twice** on the **Clock icon**. It will be minimized at the bottom of your screen.

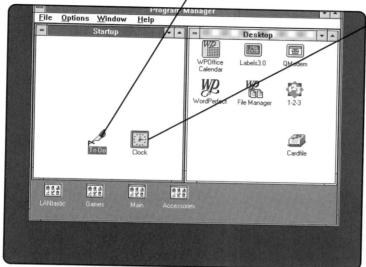

**16. Click twice** on the **Control menu box** on the left of the Startup group window title bar. The Startup group window will disappear. The Startup group icon will appear at the bottom of the Program Manager screen.

**17. Move** your customized **Desktop group window** to the **center** of the Program Manager window. You do not have to do this. However, we think it looks nicer centered on your screen. If you need help moving the window, see the section entitled "Changing the Position of a Window" in Chapter 2.

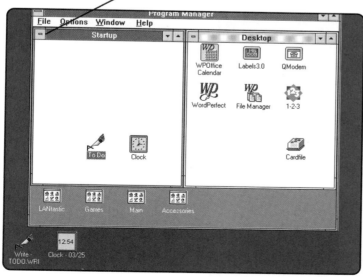

**18. Click** on **Options** in the Program Manager title bar. A pull-down menu will appear.

**19. Click** on **Save Settings on Exit.** (If the check mark is already present, click anywhere on the desktop.)

**20. Press and hold** the **Alt** key and then **press** the **F4** key (Alt + F4). The Exit Windows dialog box will appear.

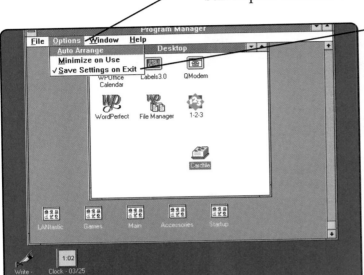

**21. Click** on **OK.** Your DOS opening screen will appear. The next time you boot up Windows, your Write To Do program and your Clock program will be booted up automatically. They will appear as minimized icons at the bottom of your screen.

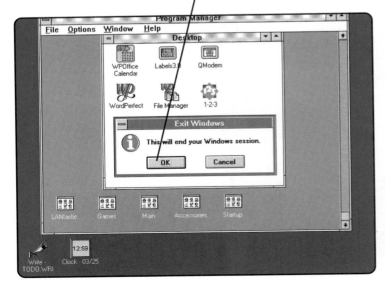

## CHANGE YOUR MIND?

You can move program icons in and out of the Startup group window at any time to meet your current work flow requirement. See Chapter 5, the section entitled "Placing Program Icons."

# Customizing Icons

If you don't like the icon that came with a particular software program or the one that was assigned to a DOS program, you can change it. Windows has three different sources of icons from which you can choose. In this chapter you will:

❖ Learn three ways to change an icon

❖ Set a program to run in minimized (icon) form

❖ Delete an unwanted icon from a group window

❖ Create a duplicate program icon in a second group window

## OPENING THE BROWSE DIALOG BOX

In this section you will change the icon for Labels 3.0 in the customized Desktop group window. If you do not have that program, you can follow the steps to change the icon for any program you wish.

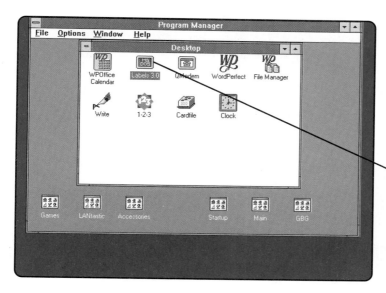

**1. Click twice** on the **Desktop group icon** at the bottom of your screen. The Desktop group window will appear. (You can change an icon in any group window.)

**2. Click once** on the **icon** you want to change. (In this example, it is Labels 3.0.) The title of the program will be highlighted.

**97**

3. **Click** on **File** in the menu bar. A pull-down menu will appear.

4. **Click** on **Properties**. The Program Item Properties dialog box will appear.

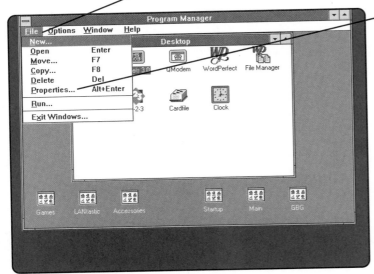

5. **Click** on **Change Icon**. The Change Icon dialog box will appear.

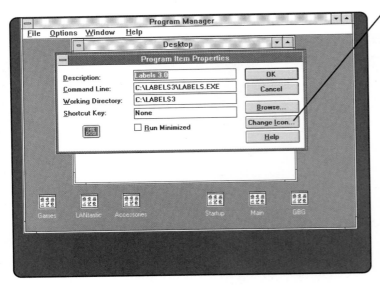

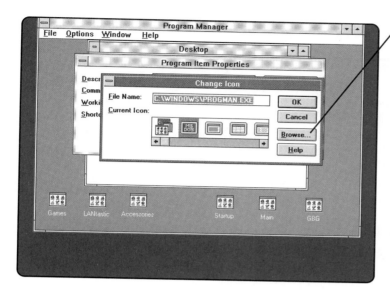

6. **Click** on **Browse**. The Browse dialog box will appear.

The Browse dialog box gives you access to three sources of icons: Program Manager icons (see the following section); More icons (see page 101); and Windows Programs icons (see page 102).

# SOURCE #1: PROGRAM MANAGER ICONS

1. **Click** on the **first item** in the File Name list box. It will be highlighted. Your list will be different depending on what software you have installed on your computer.

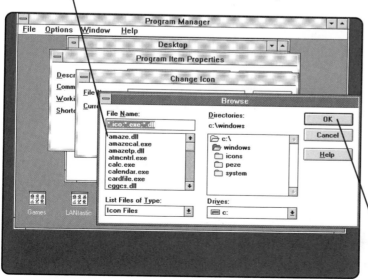

2. **Type** the letter **p**. The highlight bar will move to the first file beginning with the letter "p."

3. **Press** the **Down Arrow key** on your **keyboard** to move the highlight bar to the **PROGMAN.EXE** file if it does not appear after step 2.

4. **Click** on **OK**. The PROGMAN.EXE collection of icons will appear.

5. **Click repeatedly** on the **right arrow** to **scroll** through the available icons.

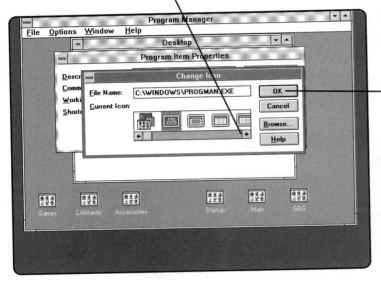

6. **Click** on the **icon** you want to assign to the Labels 3.0 program.

7. **Click** on **OK**. The Program Item Properties dialog box will appear with the new icon you chose in the lower-left corner. (If you don't want any of the icons, click on Cancel to close the dialog box.)

## SAVING THE NEW ICON

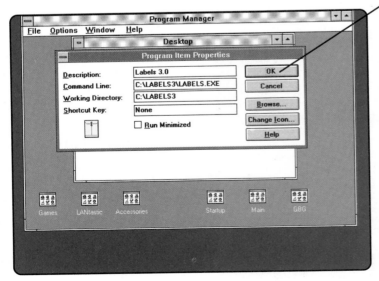

1. **Click** on **OK**. The Desktop group window will appear with the new icon.

You can minimize the Desktop group window at this point or change another icon.

In the next section, you will see a second source of icons.

# SOURCE #2: MORE ICONS

Open a group window and select an icon to change. In this section, the QModem icon in the customized Desktop group window will be changed. Refer to the section "Opening the Browse Dialog Box" on page 97 if you need help. Once you are in the Browse dialog box:

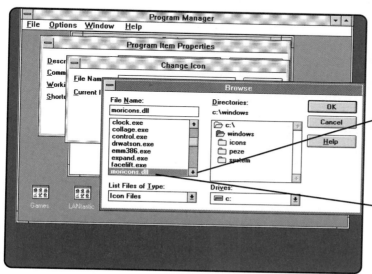

1. **Click** on the **scroll down arrow** to scroll through the list to locate the **MORICONS.EXE** file.

2. **Click twice** on **moricons.exe**. The Change Icon dialog box will appear.

3. **Click repeatedly** on the **right arrow** to scroll through the available icons.

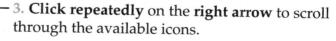

4. **Click** on the icon you want.

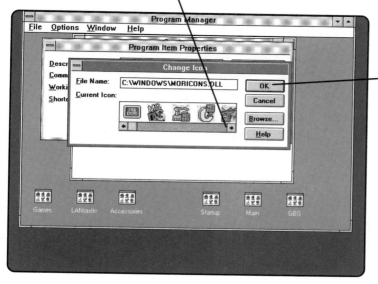

5. **Click** on **OK**. The Program Item Properties dialog box will appear with the icon you chose. (If you don't want any of the icons, click on Cancel to close the dialog box.)

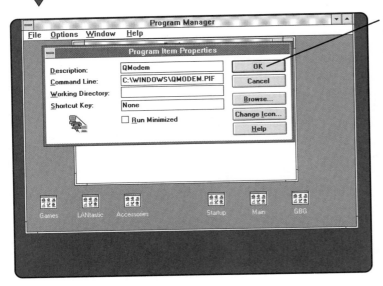

6. **Click** on **OK**. The dialog box will close and the Desktop group window will appear. The icon you chose is now in the Desktop group window.

# SOURCE #3: WINDOWS PROGRAMS ICONS

Windows has a number of programs, such as Calendar, Write, and Notepad that are part of the package.

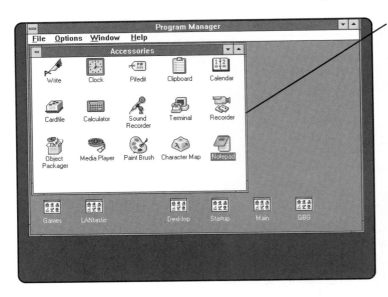

Icons for these programs are included in the Accessories group window when you install Windows. If you like one of these icons you can assign it to another program. You may have moved some of these icons to other group windows. That will not affect the steps involved in this section.

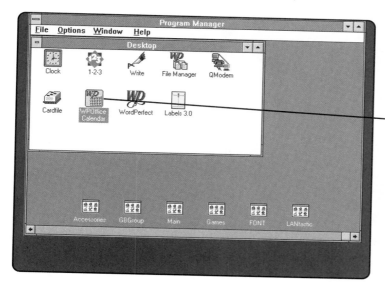

In this section you will assign the Windows Calendar icon to another calendar program.

1. Follow the steps in "Opening the Browse Dialog Box" beginning on page 97 to **change the icon** for WPOffice Calendar (or another program that you have on your computer).

Many of the EXE files listed in the Browse dialog box contain icons for the Windows programs. For example, CALC.EXE contains the icon for the Calculator program that comes with Windows; CALENDAR.EXE contains the Calendar icon; and CARDFILE.EXE contains the Cardfile icon.

2. **Click twice** on **calendar.exe**. (You can also click once, then click on OK.) The Browse dialog box will disappear and the Change Icon dialog box will appear.

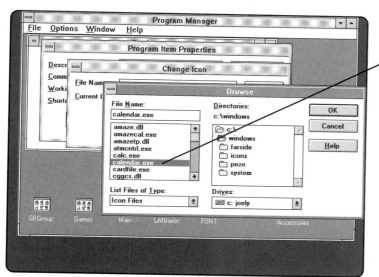

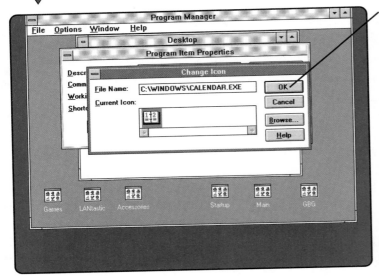

3. **Click** on **OK** in the Change Icon dialog box. It will disappear and the Program Item Properties dialog box will be on your screen displaying the newly assigned icon for the WPOffice Calendar in the lower-left corner.

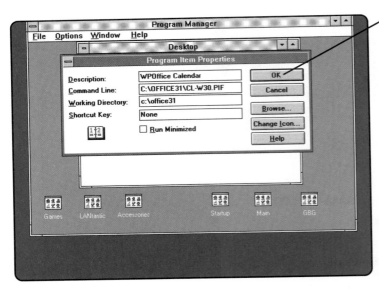

4. **Click** on **OK** to save this new selection. The icon you chose is now in your customized Desktop group window.

# CHANGING A PROGRAM NAME

In addition to changing an icon you can also change the name of a program as it appears below an icon in a group window. In this section you will change the name of WPOffice Calendar in the customized Desktop group window.

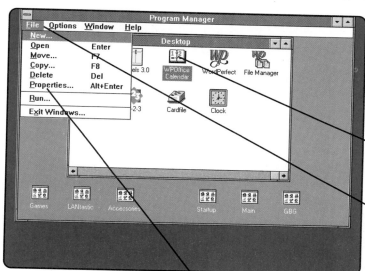

1. **Click** on the **program icon** that you want to change.

2. **Click** on **File** in the Program Manager menu bar. A pull-down menu will appear.

3. **Click** on **Properties**. The Program Item Properties dialog box will appear.

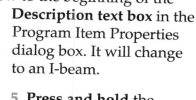

4. **Move** the mouse arrow to the beginning of the **Description text box** in the Program Item Properties dialog box. It will change to an I-beam.

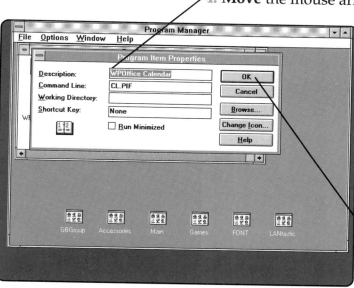

5. **Press and hold** the mouse button as you **drag** the **cursor** over the name. It will be highlighted.

6. **Type** the **new name** for the program.

7. **Click** on **OK** to save your change.

# RUNNING A PROGRAM IN MINIMIZED FORM

You can set a program so that when you boot it up it immediately goes to an icon at the bottom of your screen. In this example, you will set the Calendar to run in minimized form.

1. **Click** on the **icon** for a program that you would like to run minimized. Follow steps 1 to 3 in the previous section to open the Program Item Properties dialog box.

2. **Click** on **Run Minimized** to insert an X in the box.

3. **Click** on **OK** to save the change. Now when you boot up the Calendar program, it will be minimized to an icon at the bottom of your screen.

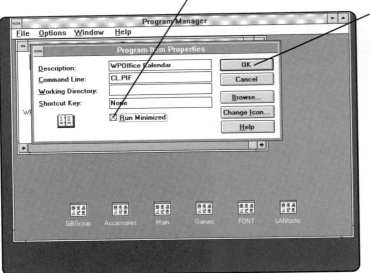

# DELETING AN ICON FROM A GROUP WINDOW

You may delete an icon from a group window if you no longer want or need it. Deleting an icon does not affect the program itself. The program is still in your computer.

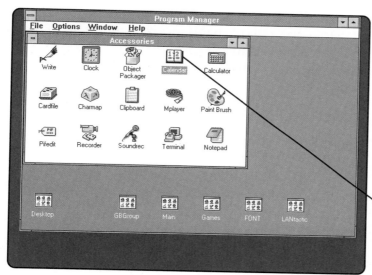

**1. Click twice** on the **Accessories group icon**. The Accessories group window will appear.

**2. Click once** on the **icon** you want to delete. In this example, the Calendar icon will be deleted.

**3. Click** on **File** in the menu bar. A pull-down menu will appear.

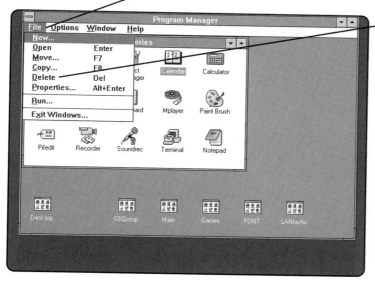

**4. Click** on **Delete**. The Delete dialog box will appear with the question, "Are you sure you want to delete item 'Calendar'?"

**5. Click** on **Yes**. The Calendar icon will be deleted from the Accessories group window.

# CREATING A DUPLICATE ICON

You can create different group windows for different functions as you learned in the section, "Opening a New Group" in Chapter 5. There may be programs, such as the Clock or Calendar, that you want to have available no matter what window you are in. In this section you will add the Clock icon to a second group window. This does not duplicate the program itself. It merely duplicates the icon that starts up the Clock program.

The process of duplicating an icon described in this section involves opening the Program Item Properties dialog box for the existing Clock program, writing down the directory and command statements, and then duplicating these statements in a new Clock setup.

1. **Click twice** on the **Accessories group icon** (or the icon for the group that contains the Clock).

2. **Click once** on the **Clock icon**. The name will be highlighted.

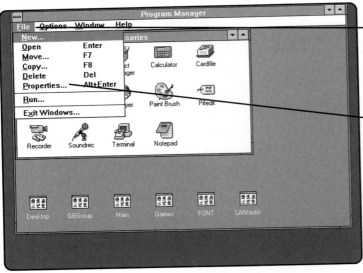

3. **Click** on **File** in the Program Manager menu bar. A pull-down menu will appear.

4. **Click** on **Properties**. The Program Item Properties dialog box will appear.

5. **Copy** down the **Description, Command Line**, and the **Working Directory** statements that you see on your screen. It is important to copy the punctuation marks and spacing exactly. In this example, there is no Working Directory line.

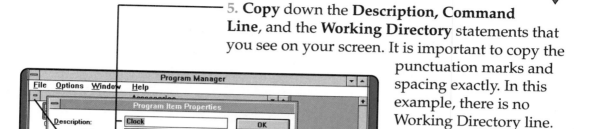

6. **Click** on **Cancel** to close the dialog box.

7. **Click twice** on the **Control menu box** on the left of the title bar in the Accessories group window (or the group window in which you are working). The group will be minimized to an icon.

8. **Click twice** on the **icon** for the group window where you would like to add the Clock. This section will show the Clock being added to the Desktop group window.

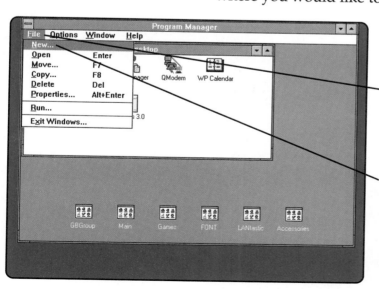

9. **Click** on **File** in the Program Manager menu bar. A pull-down menu will appear.

10. **Click** on **New**. The New Program Object dialog box will appear.

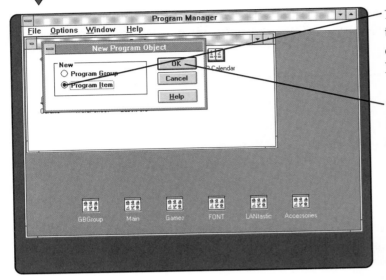

**11. Click** on **Program Item** to insert a black dot if the circle does not already have one.

**12. Click** on **OK**. The Program Item Properties dialog box will appear.

**13. Click** on the **Description text box** and **type Clock**. This is the description that will appear underneath the icon. You can type it in all capital letters if you want. You can even type a completely different description, such as MY CLOCK, if you want.

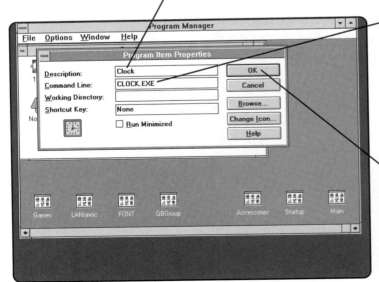

**14. Click** on the **Command Line text box** and **type** the **command statement** you copied earlier. It is important to type it exactly as it appeared in the original statement.

**15. Click** on **OK**. The clock will appear in the group window you selected.

# Customizing Colors and Patterns

The colors and patterns you see in Windows screens can be customized. In this chapter you will learn how to:

❖ Choose from a number of predesigned color schemes

❖ Create your own color scheme

❖ Choose from a number of predesigned background patterns

❖ Select a background wallpaper pattern

## OPENING THE CONTROL PANEL WINDOW

Before you can begin to customize the colors and patterns on your screen, you'll need to open the Control Panel window.

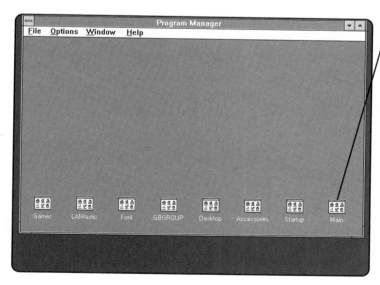

**1. Click twice** on the **Main group icon** at the bottom of your screen. It may be in a different spot than you see here. The Main group window will appear.

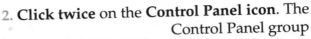

**2. Click twice** on the **Control Panel icon**. The Control Panel group window will appear on your screen.

To customize the colors you see on your screen, continue with the next sections. If you want to change the background pattern, turn to "Opening the Desktop Dialog Box" later in this chapter.

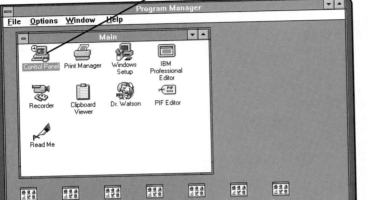

# OPENING THE COLOR DIALOG BOX

**1. Click twice** on the **Color icon**. The Color dialog box will appear on your screen.

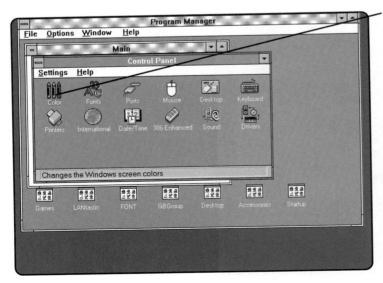

Notice that the current color scheme appears in the list box. The color scheme will be Windows Default if you are using Windows for the first time or if the colors have not been previously changed.

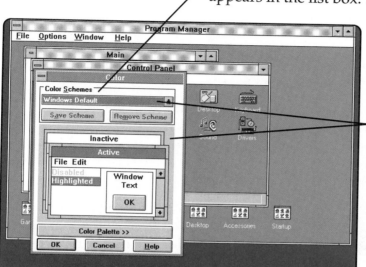

The Colors dialog box contains a sample window that displays the highlighted color scheme. In this example, the color scheme shown in the sample window is Windows Default because that is the name in the list box above.

## CHOOSING A PREDESIGNED COLOR SCHEME

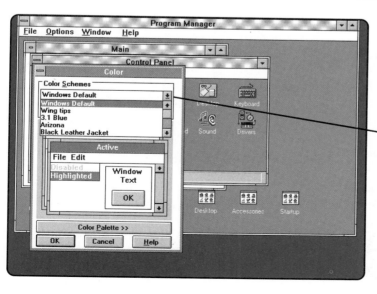

Windows 3.1 has 23 predesigned color schemes with different combinations of colors and patterns.

**1. Click** on the **down arrow** on the right of the list box. A drop-down list of color scheme choices will appear.

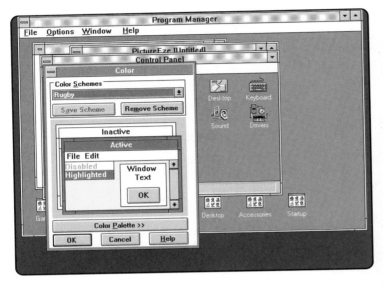

2. **Press** the **Down Arrow key** (or Up Arrow key) on your **keyboard** to move the highlight bar through the list of color schemes. As you highlight each choice, the palette in the sample window will change to show the color scheme. The color scheme shown here is Rugby.

3. When you find a color scheme you like, **click** on it. The drop-down list will disappear and the name of the color scheme you chose will be in the list box.

You can continue with the next section, "Customizing a Color Scheme." Or, if you found a color scheme you like, click on OK at the bottom of the dialog box to close it. Then follow the directions in "Returning to Program Manager" at the end of this chapter.

# CUSTOMIZING A COLOR SCHEME

You can modify a color scheme that came with Windows or create your own. In this section you will modify the Ocean color scheme.

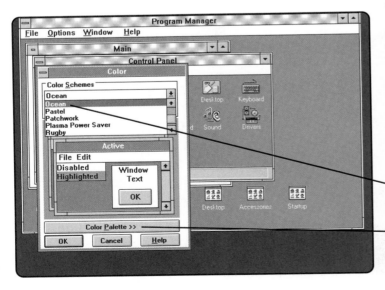

1. **Click** on **Ocean** in the Color Scheme list box.

2. **Click** on **Color Palette**. A color palette will appear on the right side of your screen.

**3. Click** on an **area** in the sample window.

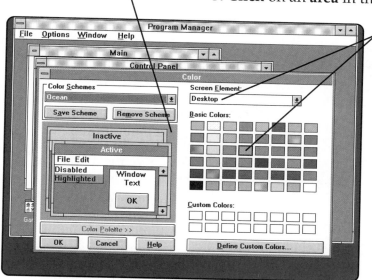

Its name will appear in the Screen Element list box. A dark border will appear around its color in the Basic Colors palette.

**4. Click** on the **color** you want to assign to that particular screen element. A dotted selection border will appear around the color, and the element in the sample window will appear in that color.

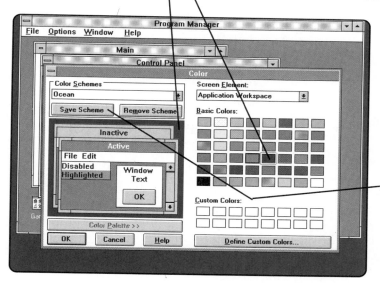

**5. Click** on **another color** and the element in the sample window will change color again.

**6. Repeat steps 3 and 4** if you want to change other screen elements.

**7. Click** on **Save Scheme**. The Save Scheme dialog box will appear.

8. **Type** a **new name** for the color scheme you have created. It will replace the name of the current scheme in the list box.

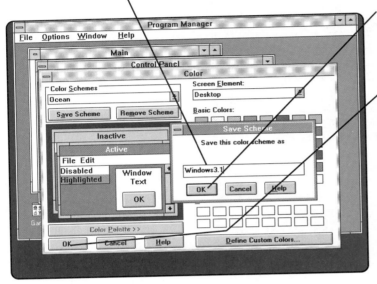

9. **Click** on **OK**. The dialog box will disappear and the new name will appear in the list of color schemes.

10. **Click** on **OK** at the bottom of the dialog box. The dialog box will disappear and the Control Panel will be on your screen.

Continue on to choose a desktop pattern. Or, go to "Returning to Program Manager" at the end of this chapter.

# OPENING THE DESKTOP DIALOG BOX

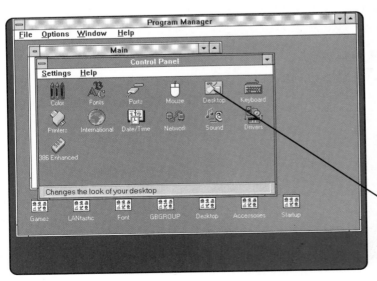

You can customize your desktop by replacing the solid color background with a pattern.

1. **Open** the **Control Panel dialog box**. See "Opening the Control Panel Window" at the beginning of this chapter if you need help.

2. **Click twice** on the **Desktop icon**. The Desktop dialog box will appear on your screen.

# CHOOSING A DESKTOP PATTERN

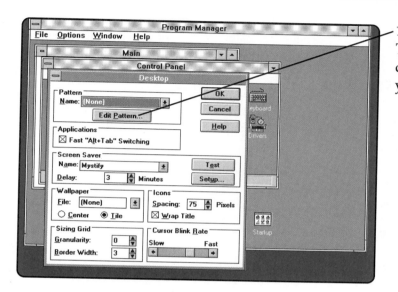

**1. Click** on **Edit Pattern**. The Desktop - Edit Pattern dialog box will appear on your screen.

**2. Press** the **Up Arrow** or **Down Arrow key** on your keyboard to scroll through the list of patterns without having to open the drop-down list. Or, **click** on the **down arrow** in the Desktop - Edit Pattern dialog box and scroll through the drop-down list.

As a pattern name appears in the list box, the pattern will be shown in the sample box. A close-up view of the pattern is also shown.

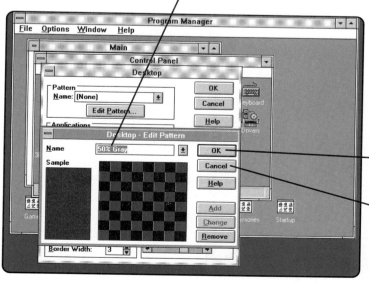

**3. Click** on **OK** when you are satisfied with a pattern.

Or, **click** on **Cancel** if you do not want a pattern.

The Desktop - Edit Pattern dialog box will disappear.

4. **Click** on **OK** to close the Desktop dialog box.

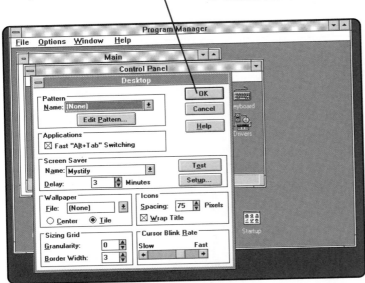

5. **Close** the **Control Panel** and **Main group windows** by **clicking twice** on the **Control menu box** on the left of each window's title bar. See the section at the end of this chapter on "Returning to Program Manager" if you need help.

# SELECTING WALLPAPER

You can further customize your desktop by selecting one of 22 dramatic patterns, called *wallpaper,* instead of a desktop pattern or color.

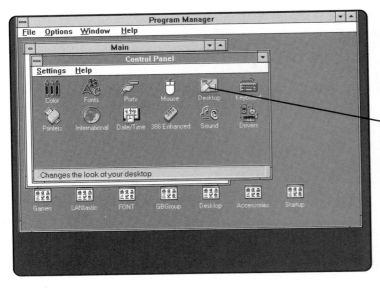

1. **Open** the **Control Panel window**. See "Opening the Control Panel Window" at the beginning of this chapter if you need help.

2. **Click twice** on the **Desktop icon**. The Desktop dialog box will appear on your screen.

**3. Move** the mouse arrow to the **Wallpaper File list box**. It will change to an I-beam.

**4. Click** on the **list box**. The text in the list box will be highlighted.

**5. Press** the **Down (or Up) Arrow key** on your keyboard to scroll through the list of wallpaper choices without having to open the drop-down list. (You cannot preview wallpaper choices.)

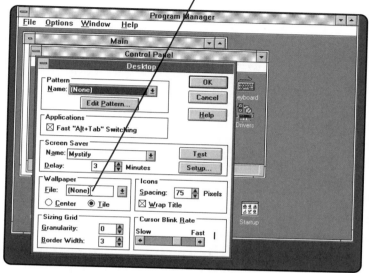

**6. Click** on **Tile** if you want the wallpaper pattern to fill your screen completely. Or, **click** on **Center** to place the wallpaper in the middle of your desktop. If you choose Center, the wallpaper pattern may be hidden behind a window on your screen.

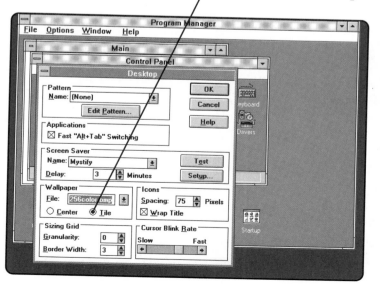

7. **Click** on **OK**. The Desktop dialog box will disappear and the wallpaper you chose will show on your screen.

If the wallpaper does not show on your screen, you must restart Windows to display your new wallpaper selection.

8. **Click twice** on the **Desktop icon** in the Control Panel to return to the Desktop dialog box. **Repeat steps 3 to 7** to see other wallpapers.

9. **Select None** in the list of choices if you do not want a wallpaper pattern.

Displaying wallpaper uses more memory than displaying a solid color or a desktop pattern.

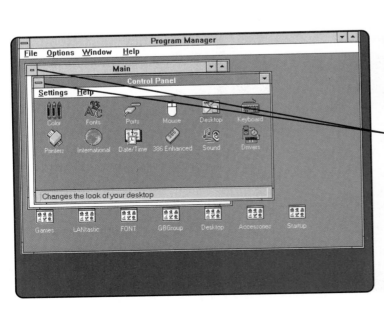

# RETURNING TO PROGRAM MANAGER

1. **Close** the **Control Panel window** by **clicking twice** on the **Control menu box** on the left of the title bar. Then **close** the **Main group window** by **clicking twice** on the **Control menu box** on the left of the Main group window title bar.

# Customizing the Screen Saver and Using Help

If you allow an image to remain on your screen for an extended period of time without any changes or movement, it may burn itself into your monitor. Windows provides a *screen saver* to guard against this. A screen saver is a constantly moving graphic image. It appears on your screen when you are interrupted in your work and don't interact with your computer for several minutes. You can customize all aspects of the screen saver. In this chapter you will:

❖ Select a screen saver pattern

❖ Customize the screen saver

❖ Learn to use Windows Help to obtain additional information about items in a dialog box

## OPENING THE DESKTOP DIALOG BOX

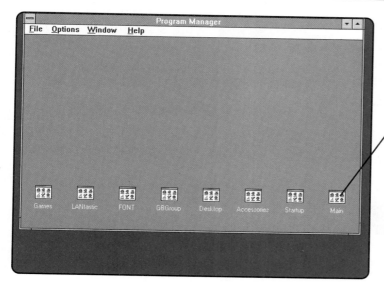

To select and customize a screen saver, you'll need to first open the Desktop dialog box in the Control Panel window.

**1. Click twice** on the **Main group icon** at the bottom of your screen. It will be enlarged and the items in the group will be shown on your screen.

2. **Click twice** on the **Control Panel icon**. The Control Panel group window will appear on your screen.

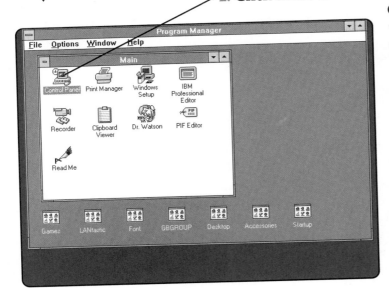

3. **Click twice** on the **Desktop icon**. The Desktop dialog box will appear on your screen.

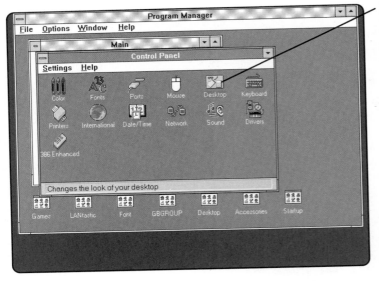

# SELECTING A SCREEN SAVER PATTERN

**1. Click** on the **down arrow** on the right of the Screen Saver Name list box. A drop-down list will appear.

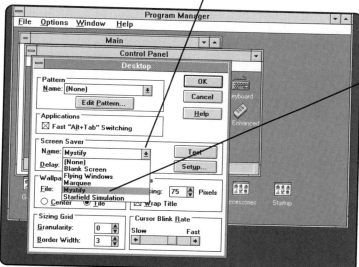

**2. Click** on **Mystify**. The drop-down list will disappear and Mystify will appear in the list box.

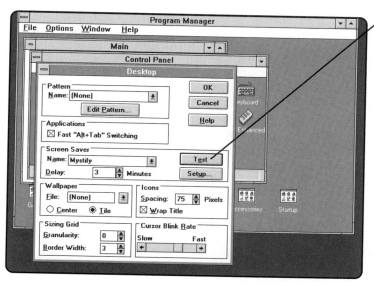

**3. Click** on **Test**. The Mystify screen saver pattern will appear on your screen.

**4. Click** to stop the test pattern and return to the Desktop dialog box.

**Repeat steps 1 to 4** to see other patterns.

**5. Click** on the **name** of the pattern you prefer.

# CUSTOMIZING THE SCREEN SAVER

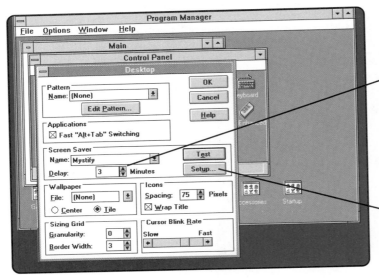

In this section you will customize the Mystify screen saver pattern.

1. **Click** on the **up arrow** to the right of the Delay list box to increase the time before the screen saver comes on. The down arrow will decrease the time.

2. **Click** on **Setup**. The Mystify Setup dialog box will appear.

3. **Click** on the **down arrow** to the right of the Shape list box. A drop-down list will appear.

4. **Click** on **Polygon 1** or **Polygon 2**. The drop-down list will disappear and your choice will appear in the list box.

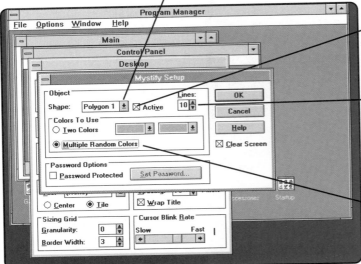

5. **Click** on **Active** to insert an X in the check box if one is not there.

6. **Click** on the **up** or **down arrow** in the Lines list box to increase of decrease the number of lines in the shape.

7. **Click** on **Multiple Random Colors** to insert a dark dot in the circle if one is not there.

**8. Click** on **Clear Screen** to insert an X in the check box if one is not there. This will clear your screen before the screen saver appear. Your work will not be

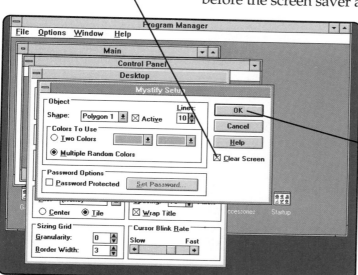

affected. The screen saver will appear against a black background. To superimpose the screen saver over your work, leave the box empty.

**9. Click** on **OK**. The Mystify Setup dialog box will disappear. The Desktop dialog box will be on your screen.

See the following section to customize other patterns.

# USING WINDOWS HELP

Every dialog box in Windows has a Help button. This button gives you access to a library of information about the topics in the dialog box. In this section you will use

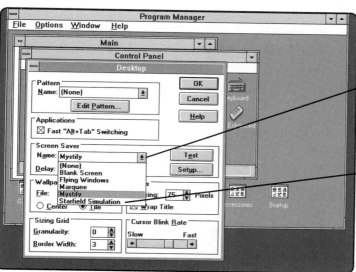

the Help button to get additional information about a screen saver pattern.

**1. Click** on the **down arrow** to the right of the Screen Saver Name list box. A drop-down list will appear.

**2. Click** on **Starfield Simulation** (or any other choice you prefer). The list will disappear and the name will appear in the list box.

3. **Click** on **Setup**. The Starfield Simulation Setup dialog box will appear.

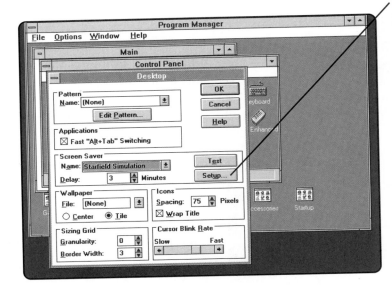

4. **Click** on **Help**. The Control Panel Help dialog box will appear.

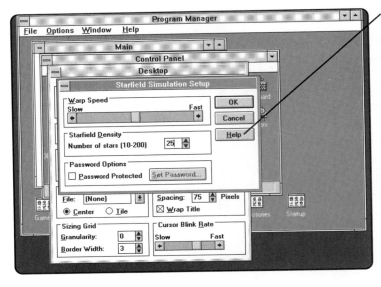

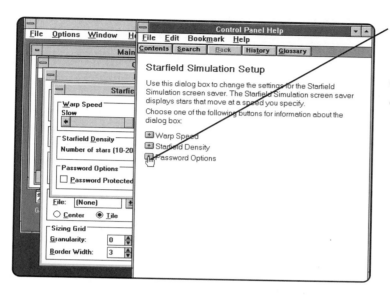

5. **Move** the mouse arrow to the **check box** beside Password Options. The arrow will change to a hand.

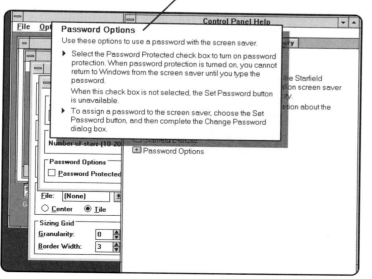

6. **Click** on the **check box**. A window containing information about Password Options will appear. It may appear in a different place on your screen.

7. **Click anywhere** on the screen to close the information window.

**Repeat steps 5 to 7** to see additional information about the other items in the Control Panel Help dialog box.

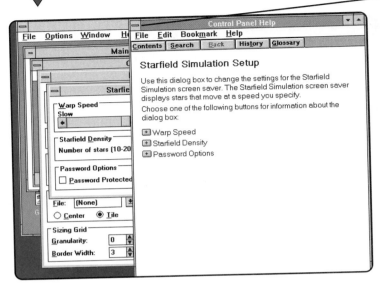

8. **Click twice** on the **Control menu box** on the left of the Control Panel Help title bar. The dialog box will disappear.

The process of using the Control Panel Help feature works the same way in every dialog box. It is an easy way to get additional information about topics in the dialog box in which you are working.

# RETURNING TO PROGRAM MANAGER

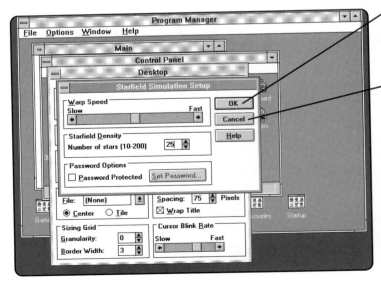

1. **Click** on **OK** to save all the settings you made in this dialog box.

Or, **click** on **Cancel** if you do not want to make changes to your current setup.

The Starfield Simulation Setup dialog box will disappear and the Desktop dialog box will be on your screen.

**2. Click** on **OK** to confirm any changes you made in this dialog box. The Desktop dialog box will disappear and the Control Panel and Main group windows will be on your screen.

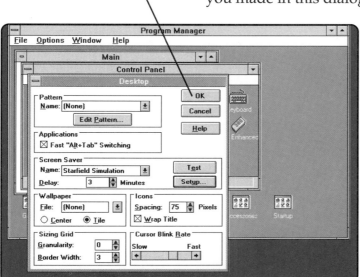

**3. Close** the **Control Panel window** by **clicking twice** on the **Control menu box** on the left of the title bar. Then **close** the **Main group window** by **clicking twice** on the **Control menu box** on the left of the Main group window title bar.

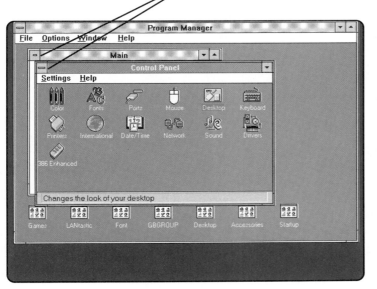

When the screen saver pattern is on your screen, simply moving your mouse will turn off the screen saver. Clicking your mouse will also turn off the screen saver.

# Customizing Your Mouse

You can customize the way your mouse works. In this chapter you will:

❖ Customize the speed of the mouse arrow

❖ Customize the speed of the double-click

❖ Switch the functions of the left and right mouse buttons (if appropriate for you)

## OPENING THE MOUSE DIALOG BOX

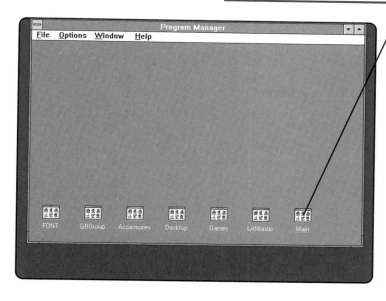

1. **Click twice** on the **Main group icon** at the bottom of your screen. The Main group window will appear.

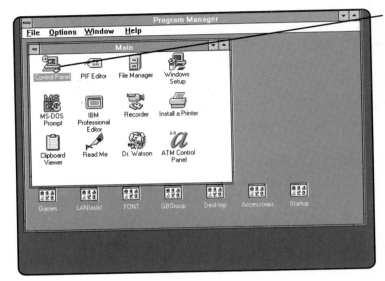

2. **Click twice** on the **Control Panel icon**. The Control Panel group window will appear on your screen.

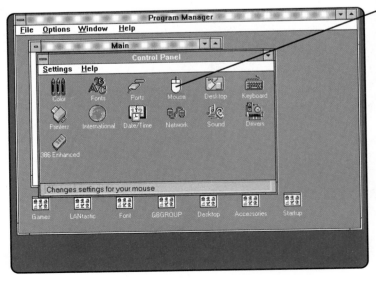

3. **Click twice** on the **Mouse icon**. The Mouse dialog box will appear on your screen.

# CUSTOMIZING THE SPEED OF THE MOUSE ARROW

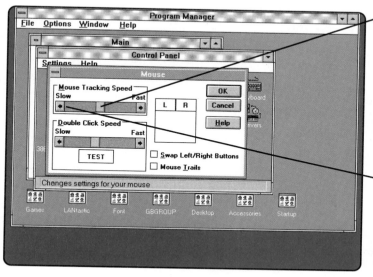

**1. Move** the mouse arrow to the scroll box on the Mouse Tracking Speed bar.

**2. Press** and **hold** the left mouse button as you **drag** the **scroll box** to the **right** to make the arrow move faster or **left** to make it slower.

Or, **click** the **Fast** or **Slow arrow** to move the scroll box.

If you do not want to make any other changes to your mouse, see "Returning to Program Manager" later in this chapter.

# CUSTOMIZING THE SPEED OF THE DOUBLE-CLICK

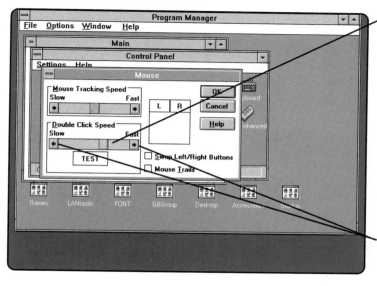

**1. Move** the mouse arrow to the **scroll box** in the Double Click Speed bar.

**2. Press** and **hold** the left mouse button as you **drag** the **scroll box** to the **right** to make the double-click register faster. **Drag** the **scroll box** to the **left** to make the double-click register slower.

Or, **click** on the **Fast** or **Slow arrow** to move the scroll box.

3. **Click twice** on the **TEST button**. If Windows recognizes the double-click, the TEST button will change to black.

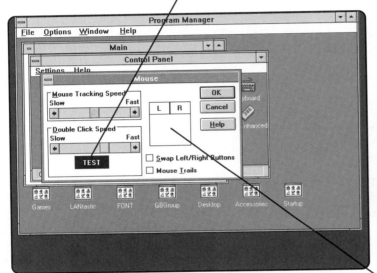

If the TEST button does not change color, decrease the speed of the double-click.

As you continue to test the acceptance of the double-click, the TEST button will change from black to white to black, etc. The actual color of the TEST button is not important. It is only important that the color change when you click twice on it.

Notice that the mouse diagram flickers on the left or right side as you press the corresponding button on your mouse.

If you do not want to make any other changes to your mouse, see "Returning to Program Manager" later in this chapter.

# SWITCHING THE LEFT AND RIGHT MOUSE BUTTONS

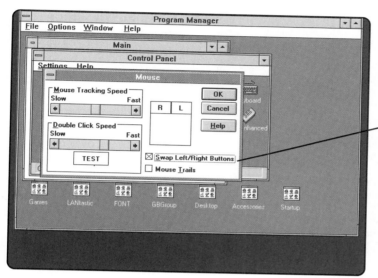

If you are left-handed, you may find operating the mouse easier if you switch the functions of the left and right mouse buttons.

**1. Click** on **Swap Left/Right Buttons** to insert an X in the check box. Notice that the mouse diagram has changed the position of the right and left buttons to reflect the switch.

The switch takes effect *immediately,* so in step 1 below you must click the right mouse button to choose OK.

If you want to go back to the standard left/right setup, click on the box (using the right mouse button) to remove the X.

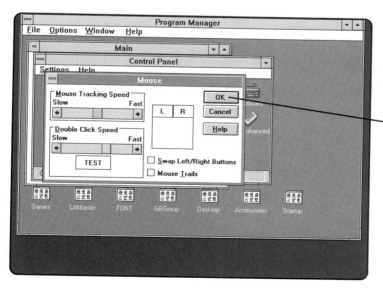

# RETURNING TO PROGRAM MANAGER

**1. Click** on **OK** to confirm any changes to your mouse. The Mouse dialog box will disappear and the Control Panel group window will appear on your screen.

2. **Click twice** on the **Control menu box** on the left of the title bar to **close** the **Control Panel window**. Then **click twice** on the **Control menu box** to **close the Main group window**. The Program Manager window will be on your screen.

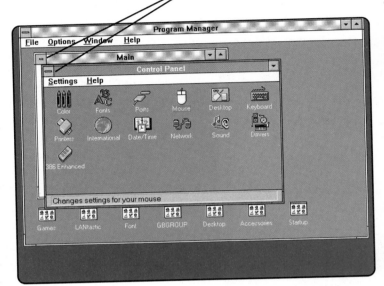

# Program Manager

## Part III: Printing

# Changing Your Primary Printer

If you purchased a new printer after installing Windows 3.1, this chapter will show you how to install it. If you have more than one printer, this chapter will show you how to select the printer you want to serve as your primary (*default*) printer. In this chapter you will:

❖ Install a printer

❖ Select a primary (default) printer

## OPENING THE CONTROL PANEL

Before you can install a printer or select or change your primary (default) printer, you must open the Printers dialog box that is located in the Control Panel.

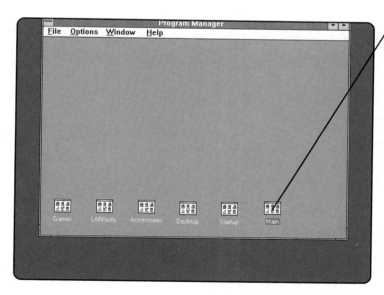

**1.** **Click twice** on the **Main group icon** at the bottom of your screen. The Main group window will appear. It may be a different size or in a different location than the one you see in the next step.

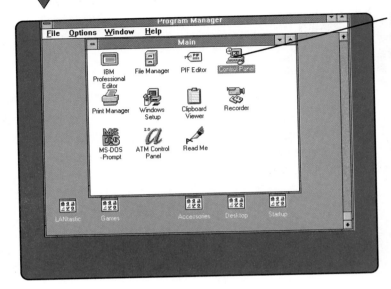

2. **Click twice** on the **Control Panel icon**. The Control Panel window will appear.

# OPENING THE PRINTERS DIALOG BOX

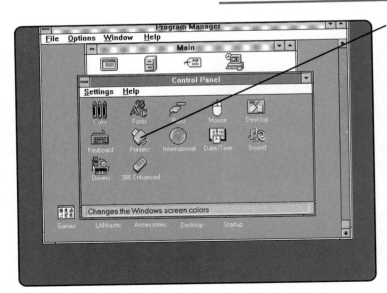

1. **Click twice** on the **Printers icon**. An hourglass will appear briefly. The Printers dialog box will appear. It may be in a different location than the one you see in the next section.

# INSTALLING A PRINTER

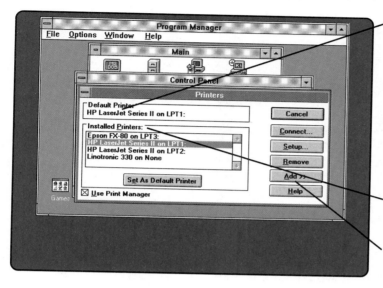

Notice the printer that is currently your default printer. (Your primary or default printer may be different.) A default printer is the one that is automatically assigned to print files in Windows-based programs.

Notice the list of printers that are currently installed.

**1. Click** on **Add**. An hourglass will appear briefly. The dialog box will expand to show the List of Printers box. It shows a list of printers you can install.

**2. Scroll** down the long list of printers using the **down arrow** on the scroll bar until you find the printer you want to install. (Click once on the arrow to move down one line. Press and hold the left mouse button on the arrow to move down the list rapidly.)

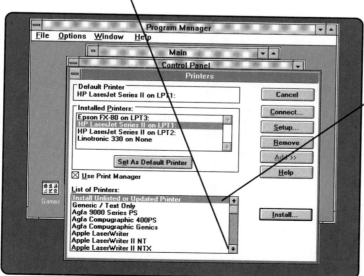

If you have a printer driver disk for your printer, select the Install Unlisted or Updated Printer option. If the printer you want to install is not on the list, you can substitute the name of another printer that your printer emulates. Many laser printers emulate the HP LaserJet II or III series.

**3. Click** on the **name of the printer** you want to install. In this example it is the Okidata OL-400.

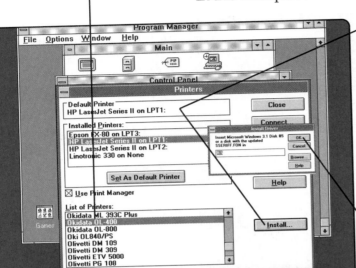

**4. Click** on **Install**. An hourglass will appear briefly. The Install Driver dialog box will appear. It will tell you which Windows 3.1 disk to insert in drive A of your computer.

**5. Insert** the specified **disk** in drive A.

**6. Click** on **OK**. The hourglass may appear and then disappear along with the dialog box.

Notice that the Okidata OL-400 printer is now on the list of installed printers. Even though the printer is installed, you cannot print with it until you select it in the print mode of a specific software program or until you select it as the default printer. The next section shows you how to reset the default printer.

**7. Click** on **Connect**. The Connect dialog box will appear.

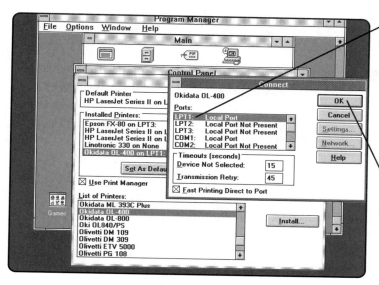

8. **Click** on **LPT1**. LPT1 is normally the communications port used for printing. If your computer has been set up to print through a different port, select that port instead.

9. **Click** on **OK**. The dialog box will disappear and the newly installed printer will be listed as set up to print through the LPT1 port. If you want your newly installed printer to be the default printer, go on to the next section. If you do not want your newly installed printer to be the default printer, go on to step 1 on the next page.

# CHANGING THE DEFAULT PRINTER

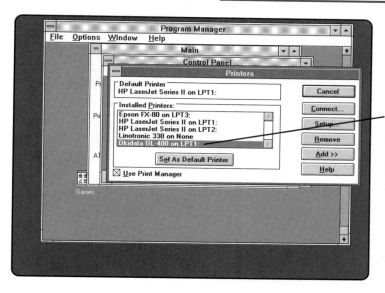

1. **Open** the **Printers dialog box**. If you need help, see the first two sections in this chapter.

2. **Click** on **Set As Default Printer**. The newly installed printer (in this case the Okidata OL-400) is now the default printer.

# RETURNING TO PROGRAM MANAGER

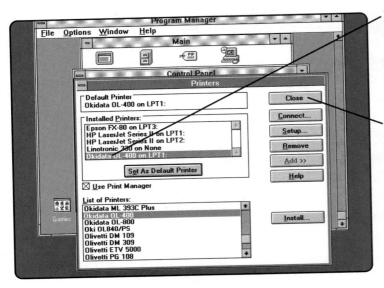

Notice that the Okidata OL-400 printer is now listed as the default (primary) printer if you changed it in the previous section.

1. **Click** on **Close**. The Printers dialog box will disappear and the Control Panel window will appear in the foreground.

2. **Click twice** on the **Control menu box** on the left of the Control Panel title bar. The Control Panel window will disappear and the Main group window will appear in the foreground. Next, **click twice** on the **Control menu box** on the left of the Main group window will disappear and you will be returned to the Program Manager window.

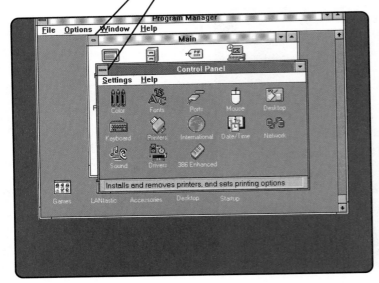

Congratulations! You have installed another printer and have changed your primary (default) printer. The printer you chose as your default printer will be used to print in all of your Windows-based software programs. You can, however, change your default printer at any time.

# Basic Printer Settings

To print a document from any Windows-based software program, you must provide specific information for the computer so that it can send the correct printing messages to the printer. Providing this information to Windows 3.1 is called *configuring* your printer. In this chapter you will provide Windows with the following information so that your printer will print the way you want it to:

❖ The print quality you want to use

❖ The size of the paper you plan to print on

❖ The amount of memory your printer has available

## OPENING THE PRINTERS DIALOG BOX

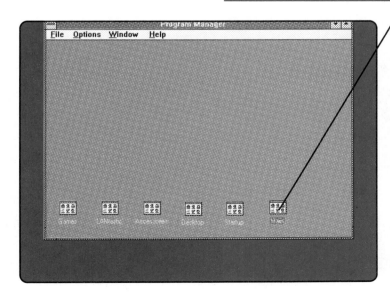

**1. Click twice** on the **Main group icon** at the bottom of your screen. The Main group window will appear. The Main group window may be a different size or in a different location than the one you see in the next step.

**2. Click twice** on the **Control Panel icon.** It may be located in a different spot in your Main group window. The Control Panel window will appear.

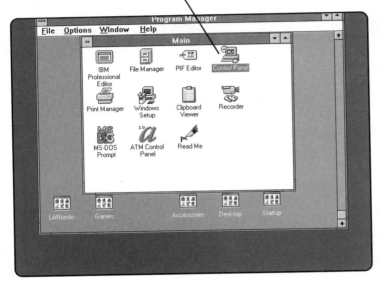

**3. Click twice** on the **Printers icon**. The Printers dialog box will appear. It may be located in a different spot on your screen.

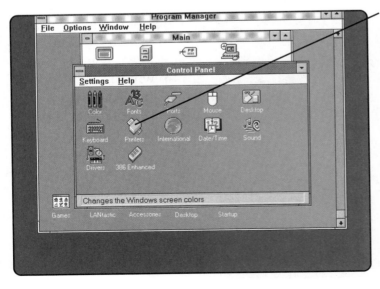

# SETTING THE PRINTER'S RESOLUTION

You can set the quality of the print on a document (as well as the speed at which it prints) by telling Windows how many dots per inch (*dpi*) you want the printer to use. The more dots per inch, the higher the resolution and quality of the print, and the slower the printing speed. Most people use 300 dpi, which is considered letter quality. Draft quality printing is 150 dpi. For very fast printing and poor quality, choose 75 dpi.

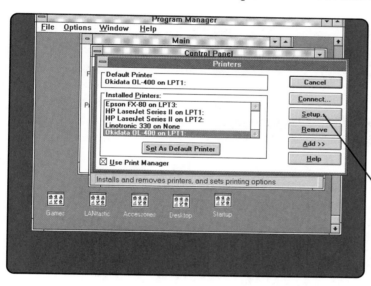

**1. Click** on **Setup**. In this example, the Okidata OL-400 dialog box will appear because this is the printer we chose. If you have selected a different printer to install, the dialog box will contain the name of the printer you selected.

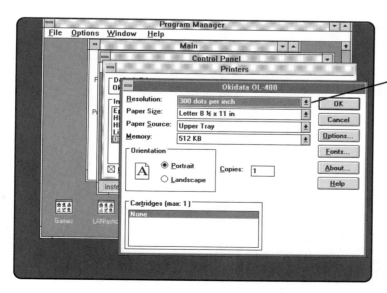

**2. Click** on the **down arrow** on the Resolution list box. A drop-down list will appear.

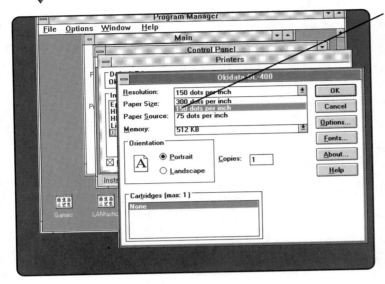

3. **Click** on the appropriate **printer resolution**. The drop-down list will disappear and the Resolution list box will reappear. In this example, the choice is 150 dpi for fast draft printing. If you have a dot matrix printer, the resolution choices will differ. In that case, click on the resolution that you want to use most often. Check your printer manual for the recommended dpi.

# SELECTING PAPER SIZE

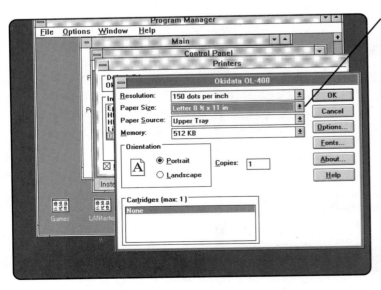

1. **Click** on the **down arrow** in the Paper Size list box. A drop-down list will appear.

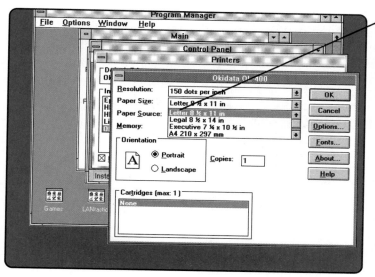

2. **Click** on the appropriate **paper size**. The drop-down list will disappear and the Paper Size list box will reappear. In this example, the choice is Letter 8 1/2 x 11, which is the standard business size in the United States. If you have a dot matrix printer, your list of paper sizes may be different.

# SETTING YOUR PRINTER'S MEMORY

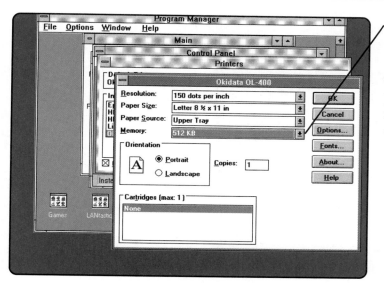

1. **Click** on the **down arrow** on the Memory list box. A drop-down list will appear. (If you have a dot matrix printer, your printer will not offer memory choices. Go on to the next section.)

2. **Click** on the appropriate **memory capacity** of your printer. The drop-down list will disappear and the Memory list box will reappear. In this example, Okidata OL-400 has 1.5MB of memory. The memory capacity of your printer may be different.

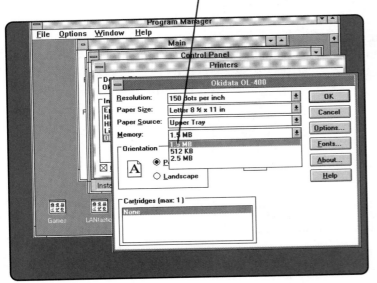

# RETURNING TO PROGRAM MANAGER

1. **Click** on **OK**. The Printers dialog box will appear in the foreground.

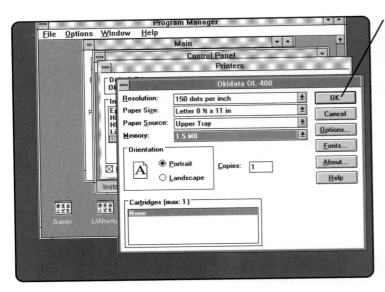

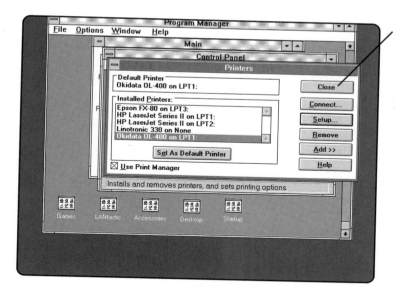

**2. Click** on **Close**. The Printers dialog box will disappear. The Control Panel window will appear in the foreground.

**3. Click twice** on the **Control menu box** on the left of the Control Panel title bar. The Control Panel window will disappear and the Main group window will appear in the foreground. Next, **click twice** on the **Control menu box** on the left of the Main group window title bar. The Main group window will disappear and you will be returned to the Program Manager window.

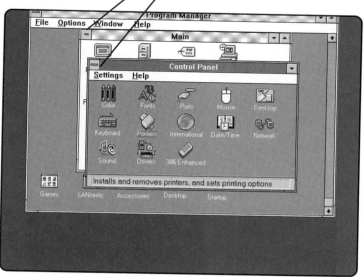

# Installing Fonts

Windows 3.1 installs fonts automatically when you install the program. *Font* is the word used to describe a specific type style. For example, most of the text of this book is typeset in a font called Palatino. If you want to install additional fonts you may do so by following the procedures in this chapter. In this chapter you will:

❖ Install part of a font family

## OPENING THE
## FONTS DIALOG BOX

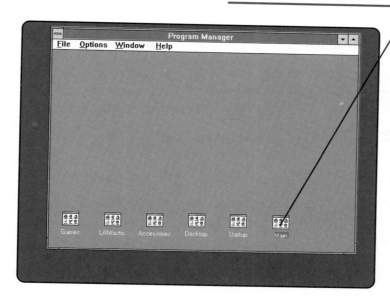

1. **Click twice** on the **Main group icon** at the bottom of your screen (the Main group icon may be in a different location on your screen). The Main group window will appear.

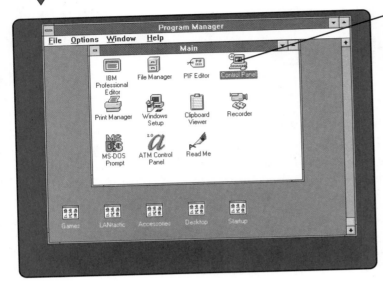

2. **Click twice** on the **Control Panel icon**. The Control Panel window will appear.

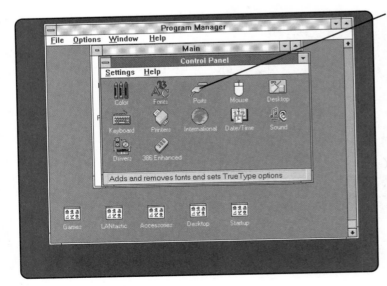

3. **Click twice** on the **Fonts icon**. The Fonts dialog box will appear.

# INSTALLING FONTS

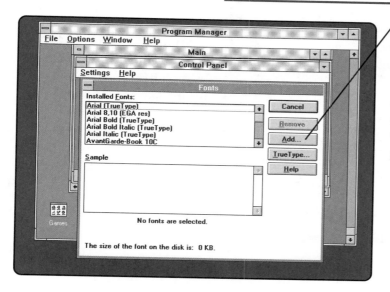

**1. Click** on **Add**. The Add Fonts dialog box will appear.

**2. Insert** the **disk** containing the fonts you want to install in drive A (or drive B).

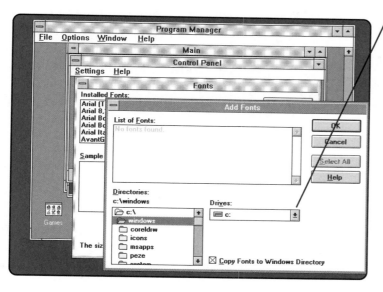

**3. Click** on the **down arrow** on the Drives list box. A drop-down list will appear.

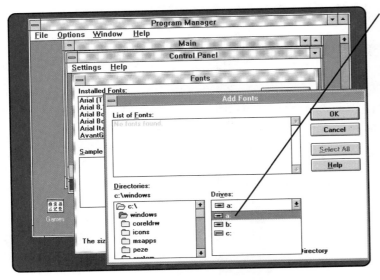

**4.** **Click** on **a:** (or the drive where you inserted your font disk). The drop-down list will disappear and the "a:" will appear highlighted in the Drives list box. An hourglass will appear for a moment. Then Windows will begin retrieving the names of the fonts that are stored on the disk in drive A.

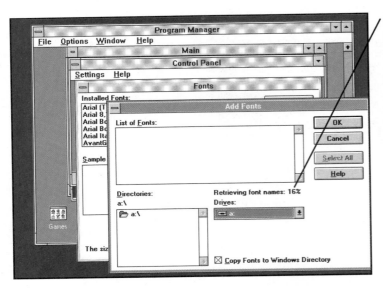

Notice that Windows tells you the percentage of the fonts being retrieved from drive A. When it has retrieved all the names, the List of Fonts dialog box will display the names of the fonts it found on drive A.

Notice the list of available fonts on the disk in drive A.

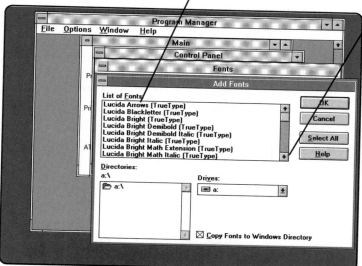

**5. Click** on the **down arrow** on the scroll bar to scroll down the list of available fonts. You may want to refer to the documentation that came with your fonts to determine which ones you want to install at this time. Your font options may be different from the ones shown in the example here. Also, if you are installing certain types of fonts, such as Adobe fonts, the installation method will be different. Consult your font software manual.

**6. Click** on the names of the **fonts** you want to install to highlight them. If you want to install more than one font, **press and hold** the **Ctrl** key as you **click** on each font. If you want them all, **click** on **Select All**.

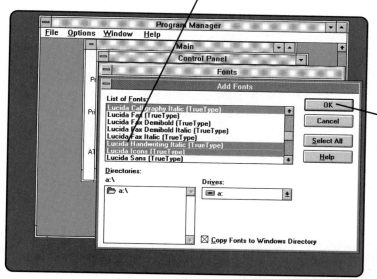

**7. Click** on **OK**. The Fonts dialog box will appear and the hourglass may appear. Each font that you selected will be added to the list of installed fonts in the Fonts dialog box. This may take a few moments depending on how many fonts you selected to install.

# CLOSING THE FONTS DIALOG BOX AND RETURNING TO PROGRAM MANAGER

Notice the highlighted list of newly installed fonts.

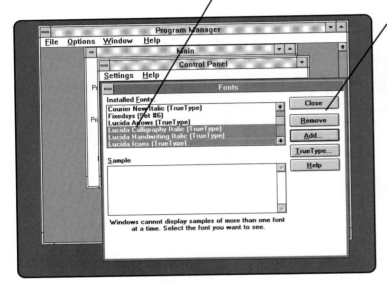

1. **Click** on **Close**. The Fonts dialog box will disappear and the Control Panel window will appear in the foreground.

2. **Click twice** on the **Control menu box** on the left of the Control Panel title bar. The Control Panel window will disappear and the Main group window will appear in the foreground. Next, **click twice** on the **Control menu box** on the left of the Main group title bar. The Main group window will disappear and you will be returned to the Program Manager window.

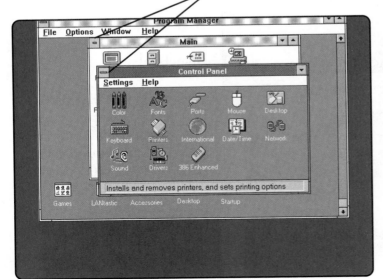

# Special Printing Options

Four of Windows' printing options (paper size, printer resolution, printer port, and printer memory capacity) are discussed in Chapter 13, "Basic Printer Settings." This chapter will use the example of changing the settings to print an envelope so you will see how to:

❖ Change paper size

❖ Select manual feed

❖ Select landscape orientation to print sideways

**Warning:** Any changes you make in these settings will affect all Windows-based programs. You can make the same changes within the Printer Setup dialog box of a specific software program. Changes made in a specific software program may or may not affect other programs.

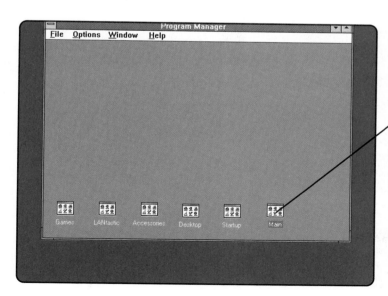

## OPENING THE PRINTERS DIALOG BOX

1. **Click twice** on the **Main group icon** at the bottom of your screen. The Main group window will appear.

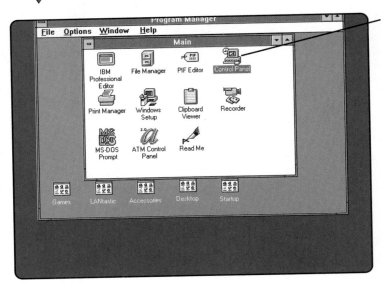

2. **Click twice** on the **Control Panel icon**. The Control Panel window will appear.

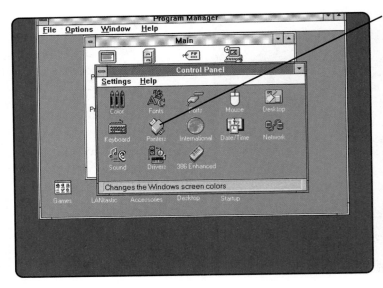

3. **Click twice** on the **Printers icon**. The Printers dialog box will appear.

# SELECTING PAPER SIZE

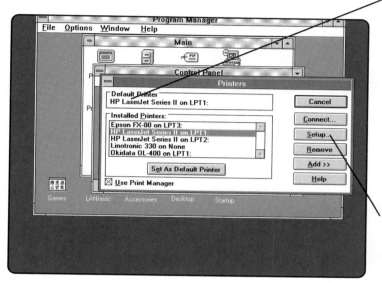

Notice that the default (primary) printer listed in this example is the HP LaserJet Series II. Your default printer may be different. If so, you may not see the same choices in the drop-down list boxes since these choices depend on the options offered by your printer.

**1. Click** on **Setup**. The dialog box for your printer will appear. In this section, it is the HP LaserJet Series II dialog box.

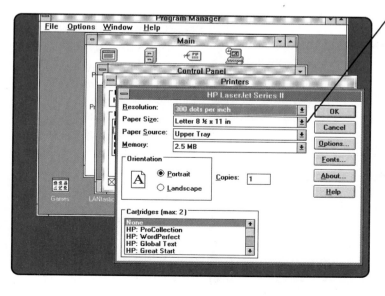

**2. Click** on the **down arrow** in the Paper Size list box. A drop-down list will appear.

3. **Click** on the **scroll down arrow** on the drop-down list box to move through the list of paper sizes.

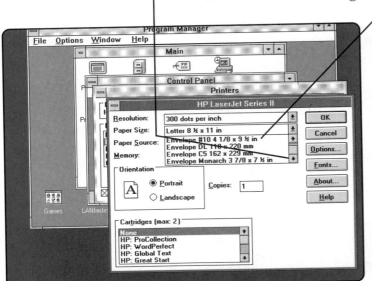

4. **Click** on **Envelope #10 4 1/8 x 9 1/2 in**. The drop-down list will disappear. The name of the envelope will appear in the Paper Size list box. This size envelope is the standard business envelope in the United States. Your paper size options will differ depending on your printer.

As you scroll through the list of paper sizes, notice the different sizes of paper your printer can use.

## SELECTING THE MANUAL FEED OPTION

The Manual Feed option is the only way you can print envelopes on an HP LaserJet Series II printer (or one that emulates an HP LaserJet Series II printer). Your printer may be different.

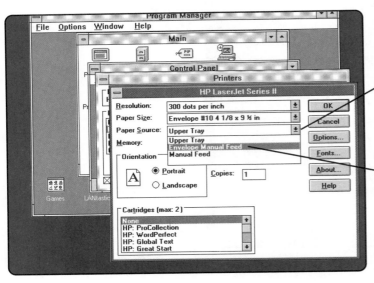

1. **Click** on the **down arrow** on the Paper Source list box. A drop-down list will appear.

2. **Click** on **Envelope Manual Feed**. The drop-down list will disappear. Envelope Manual feed will appear in the Paper Source list box.

# PRINTING SIDEWAYS (LANDSCAPE)

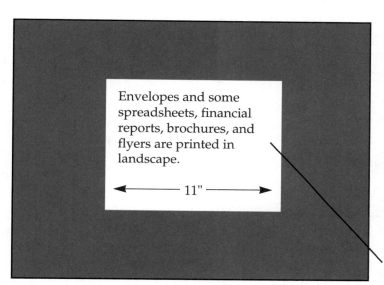

Envelopes and some spreadsheets, financial reports, brochures, and flyers are printed in landscape.

← 11" →

When you print an envelope you must print in landscape orientation. *Landscape* printing (also known as sideways printing) means printing with the long side of the paper at the top. Landscape printing is often used to print financial spreadsheets and graphs that are too wide to be printed in portrait.

This is an example of landscape printing.

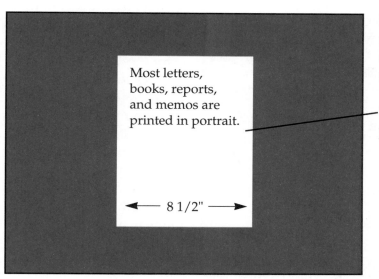

Most letters, books, reports, and memos are printed in portrait.

← 8 1/2" →

Most documents are normally printed in *portrait* orientation, with the short side of the paper at the top.

This is an example of portrait printing.

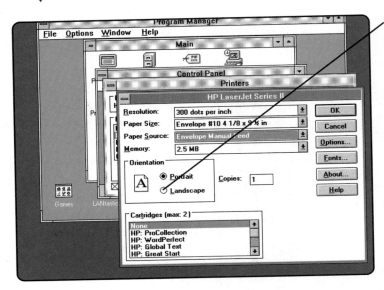

1. While you are in the HP LaserJet Series II dialog box (or the dialog box for the printer you have) **click** on the **circle** (option button) next to **Landscape** to insert a black dot. The black dot in the circle next to Portrait will disappear. Your printer is now set up to print in landscape (sideways).

# CLOSING THE PRINTERS DIALOG BOX AND RETURNING TO PROGRAM MANAGER

1. **Click** on **OK** to save any changes you made. The dialog box for your printer will disappear. The Printers dialog box will appear in the foreground. **Reminder:** If you do not want these changes in settings to affect all of your Windows-based programs, you can make the same changes in the Print Setup dialog box of a specific software program. The settings will remain in effect until you change them again.

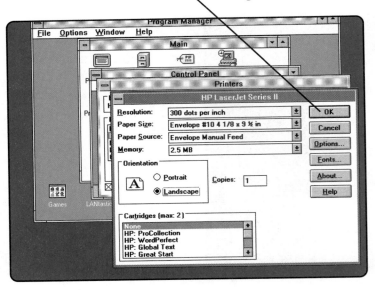

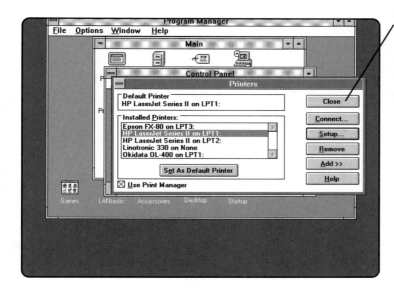

**2. Click** on **Close**. The Printers dialog box will disappear. The Control Panel window will appear in the foreground.

**3. Click twice** on the **Control menu box** on the left of the Control Panel title bar. The Control Panel window will disappear and the Main group window will appear in the foreground. Next, **click twice** on the **Control menu box** on the left of the Main group title bar. The Main group window will disappear and you will be returned to the Program Manager window.

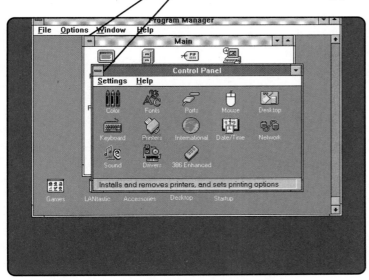

# Two Ways to Print

When you want to print several documents it can be a nuisance to open a document, print, close the document, and then open a second one, and so forth. Windows offers an ingenious solution to this repetitive process. It is called drag and drop printing. It allows you to print a file without opening it. In this chapter you will:

❖ Print a document file from within a document

❖ Print a file with the drag and drop method

## PRINTING A DOCUMENT

1. **Open** the **group window** where your Write program icon is located. If you created the customized Desktop group in Chapter 5, it is located in that group window. Or, it may be in the Accessories group window.

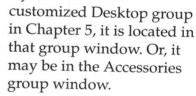

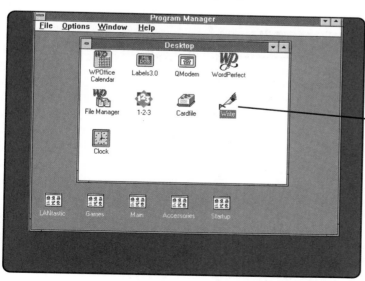

2. **Click twice** on the **Write program icon** in the group window where it is located. The Write (Untitled) window will appear.

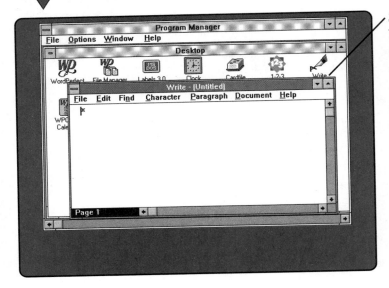

3. **Click** on the **Maximize button** (▲) on the right of the Write title bar. The window will enlarge to fill the screen. This is the ideal size for a word processing window.

4. **Type** a phrase or a **few words** so you will have something to print. To learn more about how to use the Windows Write program, see Chapter 19, "Introducing Windows Write."

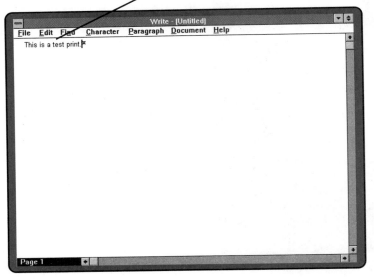

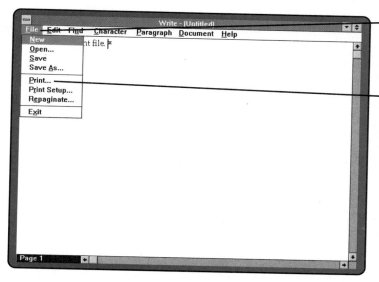

5. **Click** on **File** in the menu bar. A pull-down menu will appear.

6. **Click** on **Print**. The Print dialog box will appear. If you have already set up your printer, go on to step 7. If you need help with your printer's setup, see Chapter 13, "Basic Printer Settings," and Chapter 15, "Special Printing Options."

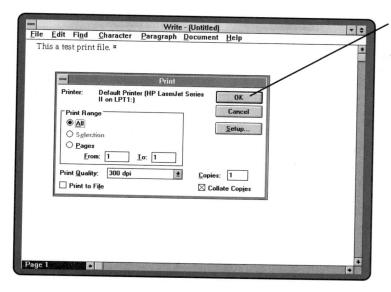

7. **Click** on **OK**. A Write dialog box will appear briefly.

Notice the Now Printing message box. Since the document contains only a few words, the box will disappear quickly. The more text in a document file, the longer this message will stay on the screen.

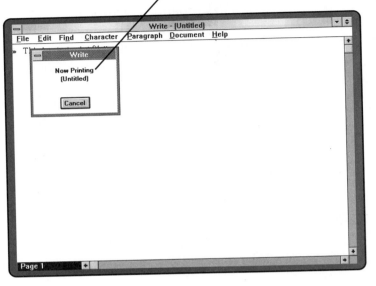

If you change your mind, **click** on **Cancel** to cancel the printing.

## QUICK EXIT

Try this method of exiting and saving a file.

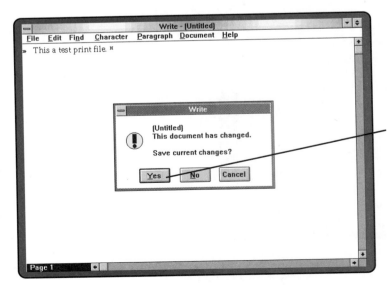

1. **Press and hold** the **Alt** key and then **press** the **F4** key (Alt + F4). The Write "Save Current Changes?" box will appear.

2. **Click** on **Yes** if you want to save the file. **Click** on **No** if you do not want to save it. The Write dialog box will disappear. The Desktop group window will appear. **Click** on **Cancel** if you want to return to the document screen.

# DRAG AND DROP PRINTING

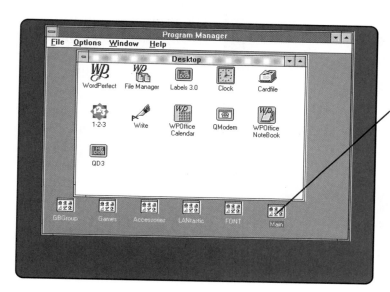

Drag and drop printing is done with the Print Manager and the File Manager.

**1. Click twice** on the **Main group icon** at the bottom of your screen. The Main group window will appear.

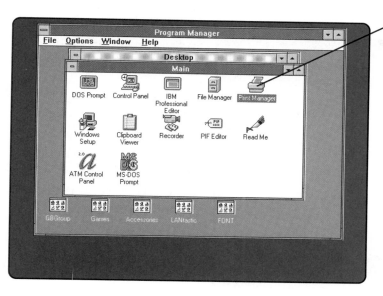

**2. Click twice** on the **Print Manager icon**. The Print Manager window will appear.

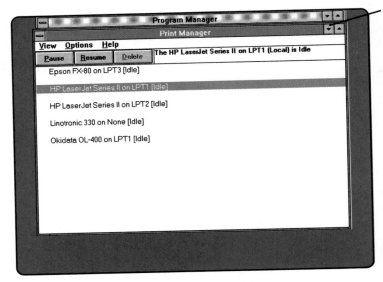

3. **Click** on the **Minimize button (▼)** on the right of the Print Manager title bar. The Print Manager icon will appear at the bottom of your screen. The Main group window will reappear.

The chances are that your Print Manager screen will not show as many installed printers as this one.

Notice the Print Manager icon at the bottom of the screen. When an icon is located at the bottom of your screen, it means it is in the computer's memory (active).

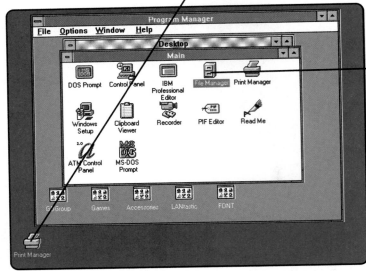

4. **Click twice** on the **File Manager icon**. The File Manager window will appear. Your File Manager window may appear in a different size and position than the example on the next page.

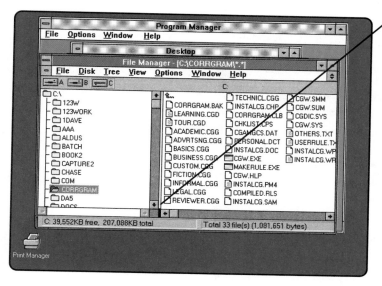

5. **Click** on the **down arrow** to scroll down the list of directories in your computer. Look for the WINWRITE directory you created in Chapter 7, "Customizing Startups" (or any directory where you have Windows Write files you want to print).

6. **Click** on **WINWRITE**. It will be highlighted and the list of files contained in that directory will be displayed in the box on the right.

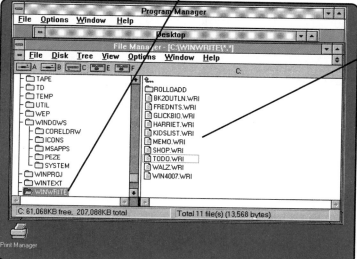

Notice the list of files contained in the WINWRITE directory. Your list may be different.

7. **Move** the mouse arrow to the **file icon** on the left of the file you want to print. In this example, the choice is TODO.WRI.

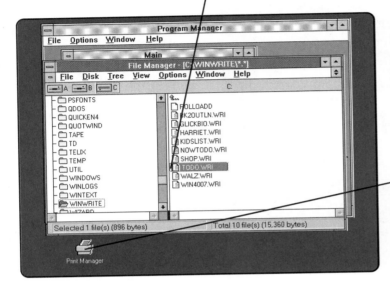

8. **Press and hold** the mouse button as you **drag** the **file icon** to the Print Manager icon at the bottom of your screen. The file icon will change briefly to a circle and then change back to a file icon.

9. **Release** the mouse button when the **file icon is on top of the Print Manager icon**. The TODO.WRI document will open and the Print dialog box will appear.

10. **Click** on **OK**. A Now Printing message box will appear. Your document will be printed and the File Manager window will reappear. You can repeat steps 7 to 10 with as many document files as you like. As you can see, drag and drop printing is a very efficient way to print many documents at one time. The only limitation is that some software programs are not capable of taking advantage of this feature.

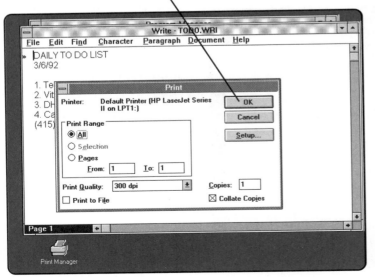

# QUICK EXIT

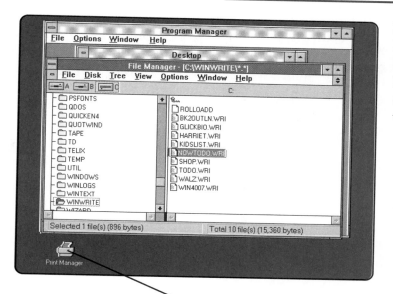

**1. Press and hold** the **Alt** key and then **press** the **F4** key (Alt + F4). The File Manager window will disappear. The Main group window will appear.

**2. Click once** on the **Print Manager icon** at the bottom of your screen. (Make certain that you only click once or the Print Manager window will open.) The pop-up Control menu will appear.

**3. Click** on **Close**. The Print Manager icon at the bottom of your screen will disappear.

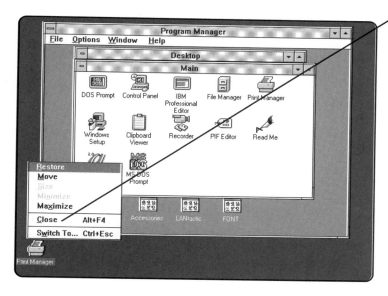

4. **Click** on the **Minimize button (▼)** on the right of the Main group window title bar. Be careful not to click on the Minimize button in the Desktop title bar. The Main group window will become an icon at the bottom of your screen. The Desktop group window (or the group window where Windows Write is located) will appear in the foreground.

# Using Print Manager

In the old days when you were printing a file you could not use your computer while a file was printing. In addition, you could send only one file to the printer at a time. Windows has solved these frustrating problems with Print Manager. When you use Print Manager, you can continue to work on your computer while it is printing a document. Moreover, you can have a number of files lined up to print automatically while you continue to work. In this chapter you will:

❖ Turn on Print Manager

❖ Set the speed at which Print Manager prints documents

❖ Use Print Manager to pause or cancel the printing of a document

## TURNING ON PRINT MANAGER

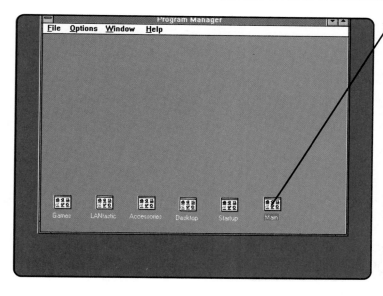

1. **Click twice** on the **Main group icon** at the bottom of your screen. The Main group window will appear.

**2. Click twice** on the **Control Panel icon**. The Control Panel window will appear.

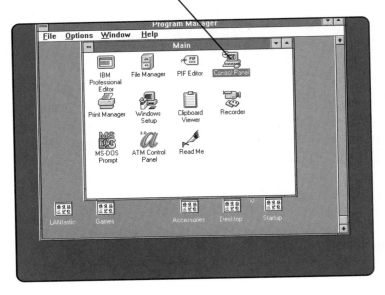

**3. Click twice** on the **Printers icon**. The Printers dialog box will appear.

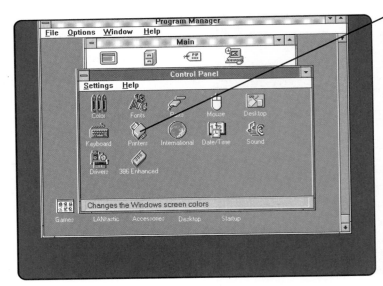

**4. Click** on the **Use Print Manager check box** to put an X in the box if one is not already there.

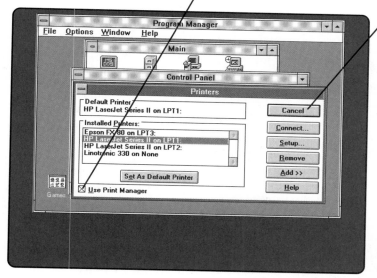

**5. Click** on **Cancel** if the X is there. If the X is not there and you have to click on the Use Print Manager check box to insert the X, the Cancel button will change to Close. **Click** on **Close** to confirm the change. The Printers dialog box will disappear and the Control Panel window will appear in the foreground.

From now on, when you print from any program in Windows, Print Manager will take charge of the printing operation. Every time you print a document the Print Manager icon will appear at the bottom of your screen while the document is printing. Once the printing operation is completed, the Print Manager icon will disappear. You can turn Print Manager off at any time by clicking on the same box to remove the X.

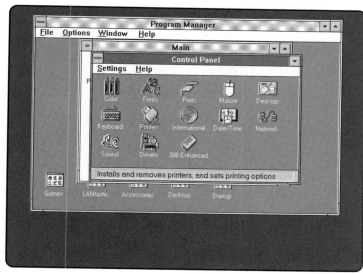

## QUICK CLOSE

**1. Press and hold** the **Alt** key and then **press** the **F4** key (Alt + F4). The Control Panel window will close and the Main group window will appear in the foreground.

In the next section, you will set the speed at which Print Manager prints your documents.

# CONTROLLING PRINT SPEED

1. **Click twice** on the **Print Manager icon**. The Print Manager window will appear. It will show a list of the printers you currently have installed to print in Windows. It will also show the printing status of each printer. If you are not printing, each printer's status will be shown as "Idle."

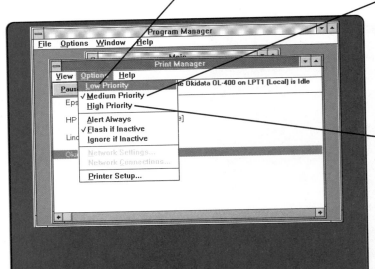

2. **Click** on **Options** in the Print Manager menu bar. A pull-down menu will appear.

3. **Click** on one of the following **Priority options** you want Print Manager to give to your printing operation:

❖ *Low Priority* means you can work at almost normal speed on your computer but printing is very slow.

❖ *Medium Priority*, the standard (default) priority, means printing is faster than low priority and your working speed in a document file is faster than high priority.

❖ *High Priority* means that memory is taken away from the computer and given to the printer. Printing is the fastest but your working speed is the slowest. Once you have clicked on a Priority, the pull-down menu will disappear.

# PAUSING A PRINT JOB

**1. Open Print Manager** and **click** on the **printer** you want to pause. It will be highlighted.

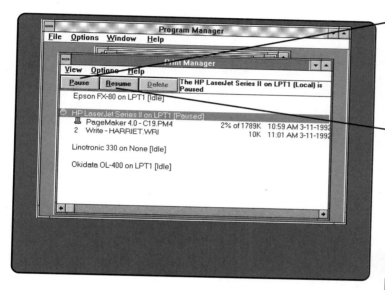

**2. Click** on **Pause**. Printing on this printer will be discontinued and a Pause icon will appear beside the printer.

**3. Click** on **Resume** to begin printing again.

# CANCELING A PRINT JOB

**1. Open Print Manager** and **click** on the **filename** you want to stop printing. It will be highlighted.

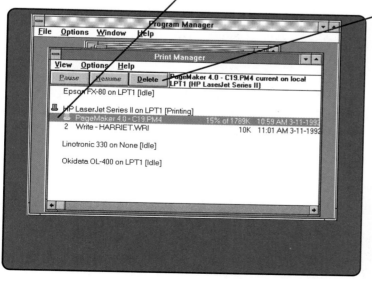

**2. Click** on **Delete**. A Print Manager dialog box will appear. It will ask "Do you want to stop printing the document?" **Click** on **Yes**. The dialog box will disappear and the document name will disappear from the list of files in the print queue. You must minimize Print Manager when you are through. Closing Print Manager will cancel all printing jobs.

# EXITING PRINT MANAGER AND RETURNING TO PROGRAM MANAGER

1. **Click** on the **Control menu box** on the left of the Print Manager title bar. A pull-down menu will appear. (Or, **press and hold** the **Alt** key and then **press** the **F4** key (Alt + F4.)

2. **Click** on **Close**. The Print Manager window will disappear. The Main group window will appear in the foreground.

**Program Manager**

File  Options  Window  Help

**Print Manager**

Restore
Move
Size
Minimize
Maximize
Close          Alt+F4
Switch To... Ctrl+Esc

The HP LaserJet Series II on LPT1 (Local) is Idle

[Idle]

LPT1 [Idle]

[Idle]

Okidata OL-400 on LPT1 [Idle]

---

3. **Click** on the **Control menu box** on the left of the Main group window title bar. A pull-down menu will appear.

4. **Click** on **Close**. The Main group window will disappear. The Program Manager screen will appear in the foreground.

**Program Manager**

File  Options  Window  Help

**Main**

Restore
Move
Size
Minimize
Maximize
Close          Ctrl+F4
Next          Ctrl+F6

PIF Editor    Control Panel

Clipboard Viewer    Print Manager

MS-DOS Prompt    ATM Control Panel    Read Me

Games    LANtastic    Accessories    Desktop    Startup

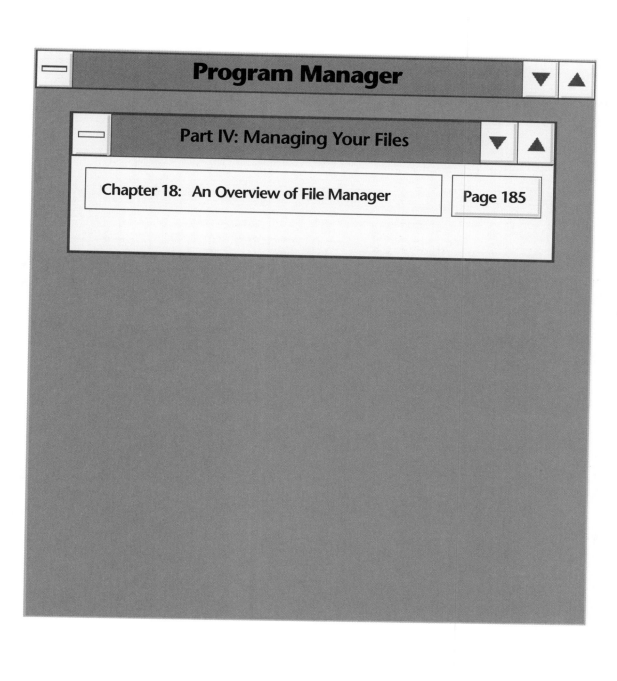

# Program Manager

## Part IV: Managing Your Files

Chapter 18:   An Overview of File Manager          Page 185

# An Overview of File Manager

If you think that copying and moving files is a boring task, wait until you try the drag and drop feature of the new and improved File Manager! You can move and copy multiple files with one procedure. You can also move back and forth between directories at the click of your mouse. Several features of File Manager have already been covered in earlier chapters. For example, making a directory is covered in Chapter 7, "Customizing Startups," and drag and drop printing is covered in Chapter 16, "'Two Ways to Print." In this overview of File Manager you will:

❖ Sort files and display file information

❖ Select files

❖ Copy files from one drive to another with drag and drop copying

❖ Move files from one directory to another with drag and drop procedures

❖ Delete files

## OPENING FILE MANAGER

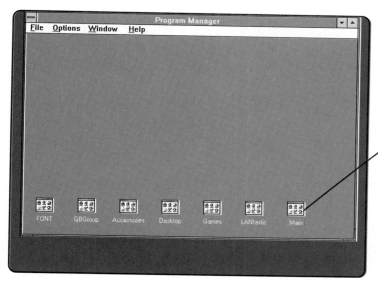

As you go through these procedures your group windows may appear in a different size or position from the examples shown here.

1. **Click twice** on the **Main group icon** at the bottom of the screen. The Main group window will appear. (You may have different icons in your Main group window.)

**2. Click** on the **File Manager icon**. The File Manager window will appear.

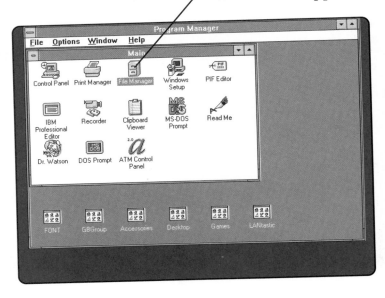

The File Manager screen may have appeared in its maximized form on your screen. If it did not, do step 3 to maximize it.

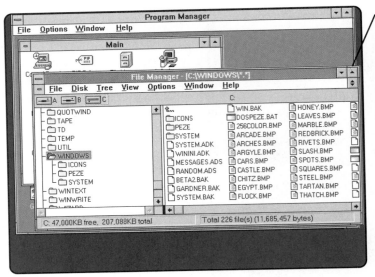

**3. Click** on the **Maximize button (▲)** on the right of the File Manager title bar. This will maximize the size of the File Manager window to fill your screen.

The left side of the File Manager window displays the *directory tree.* The directory tree shows the directories and subdirectories of the selected drive. If your File Manager screen shows only the left side of the screen with the directories and does not show the directory files on the right, go to the next section, "Changing the View."

```
File Manager - [C:\WINDOWS\*.*]
 File   Disk   Tree   View   Options   Window   Help
 A      B      C                       C:
 OFFICE31            LEAVES.BMP      CGGCS.DLL        OLDCNTRL.
 PCKWIK     ICONS    MARBLE.BMP      CGWHOOK.DLL      PACKAGER.
 PCLFONTS   PEZE     REDBRICK.BMP    MORICONS.DLL     PBRUSH.EX
 PCO        SYSTEM   RIVETS.BMP      PBRUSH.DLL       PIFEDIT.EXI
 PM4        SYSTEM.ADK  SLASH.BMP    PECORDER.DLL     PRINTMAN.
 PSFONTS    WININI.ADK  SPOTS.BMP    ATMINIB.ETA      PROGMAN.I
 QDOS       MESSAGES.ADS  SQUARES.BMP  AMAZECAL.EXE   RECORDER
 QUICKEN4   RANDOM.ADS  STEEL.BMP    ATMCNTRL.EXE     REGEDIT.E
 QUOTWIND   BETA2.BAK   TARTAN.BMP   CALC.EXE         SETUP.EXE
 TAPE       GARDNER.BAK  THATCH.BMP  CALENDAR.EXE     SMARTDRV
 TD         SYSTEM.BAK  WINLOGO.BMP  CARDFILE.EXE     SOL.EXE
 TEMP       WIN.BAK     ZIGZAG.BMP   CHARMAP.EXE      SOUNDREC
 UTIL       DOSPEZE.BAT  CALENDAR.CAL  CLIPBRD.EXE    TASKMAN.E
 WINDOWS    256COLOR.BMP  MY.CAL      CLOCK.EXE       TERMINAL.I
   ICONS    ARCADE.BMP  MAIN.CE      COLLAGE.EXE      WINFILE.EX
   PEZE     ARCHES.BMP  LMOUSE.COM   CONTROL.EXE      WINHELP.E
   SYSTEM   ARGYLE.BMP  WIN.COM      DRWATSON.EXE     WINMINE.E:
 WINTEXT    CARS.BMP    CHKLIST.CPS  EMM386.EXE       WINTUTOR
 WINWRITE   CASTLE.BMP  TEL.CRD      EXPAND.EXE       WINVER.EX
 WIZARD     CHITZ.BMP   REG.DAT      FACELIFT.EXE     WRITE.EXE
 WPC        EGYPT.BMP   WINTUTOR.DAT  MPLAYER.EXE     ACCESSOR.
 WS         FLOCK.BMP   AMAZE.DLL    MSD.EXE          ALDUS.GRF
 ZIP        HONEY.BMP   AMAZETP.DLL  NOTEPAD.EXE      APPLICAT-C
C: 45,976KB free, 207,088KB total         Total 226 file(s) (12,734,033 bytes)
```

The box around the C drive icon indicates that you were working in drive C when you booted up the File Manager and that C is the selected drive.

WINDOWS is highlighted and the file folder icon beside it is open to show that this is the directory whose files are shown in the right side of the File Manager window. Directories and files are identified with the following icons:

- 🗀  Directories and subdirectories
- ▦  Program and batch files
- 🖹  Windows document files
- 🗋  System or hidden files; non-Windows documents

See your Windows 3.1 documentation for more details about directories and files.

Notice in this example that Windows has three subdirectories listed beneath it.

If you click on any directory or subdirectory on the left, the files in the selected directory will be shown on the right.

# CHANGING THE VIEW

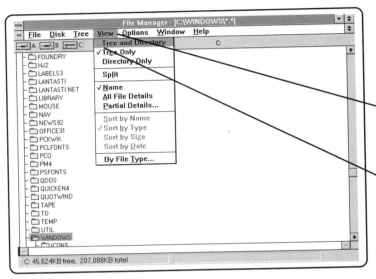

If your File Manager screen shows only the directories on the left, you can change the view to show the files in the directory.

1. **Click** on **View** in the menu bar. A pull-down menu will appear.

2. **Click** on **Tree** and **Directory**. The pull-down menu will disappear and the files in the Windows directory will appear on the right side of the screen.

# SORTING FILES

You can sort files by name, type, size, and date.

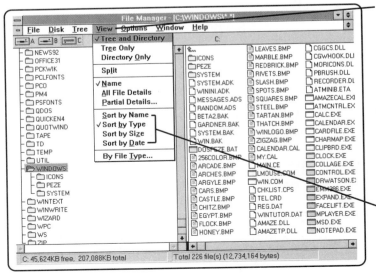

1. **Click** on **View** in the menu bar. A pull-down menu will appear.

The check mark beside Sort by Type indicates that the files in this directory are sorted alphabetically by extension (type), then by name within type.

2. **Click** on the **sort** you want. A check mark will appear beside the choice and the files will be rearranged.

# DISPLAYING FILE INFORMATION

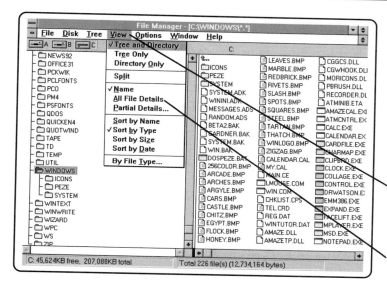

You can view information about the entire directory or selected files.

**1. Click** on the directory that you want to examine. In this example, it is WINDOWS.

**2. Click** on **View** in the menu bar. A pull-down menu will appear.

**3. Click** on **All File Details**.

The file information will appear on the right side of the File Manager window.

File information includes the filename, the number of bytes in the file, the date and time of the last modification, and a file attribute abbreviation. File attributes are assigned by DOS.

In this example, "A," the abbreviation for "Archive," indicates that the file has been modified. Consult your Windows 3.1 documentation if you would like more details about file attributes.

**4.** To show the file listing as it was, **click** on **View** in the menu bar.

**5. Click** on **Name**. Only the filenames will be shown.

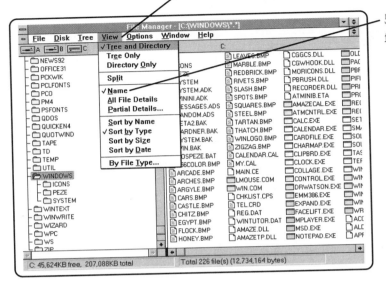

# SELECTING FILES

In order to copy or move files you must first select (highlight) them. You can select a single file, a block of files, or many single files.

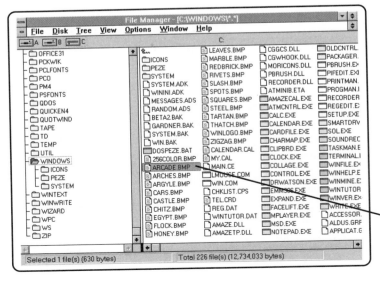

## Selecting a Single File

**1. Click** on **any file**. It will be highlighted.

# Selecting a Block of Files

**1. Click** on the **first file** in the block of files you want to select. It will be highlighted.

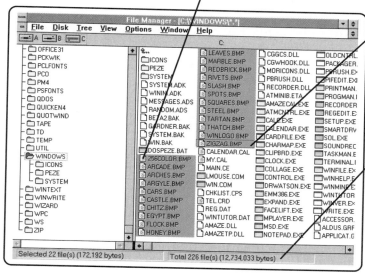

**2. Press** and **hold** the **Shift key**. Then **click** on the **last file** you want to select. The entire list of files between the two files you clicked on will be highlighted.

Notice the information about the selected files and the selected drive displayed at the bottom of your screen.

# Selecting Many Single Files

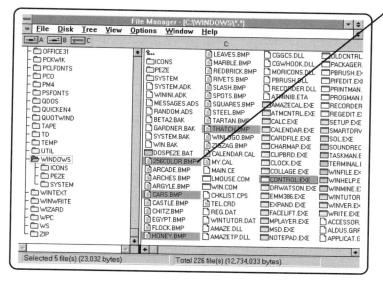

**1. Click** on the **first file** you want to select. It will be highlighted.

**2. Press and hold** the **Ctrl** key. Then **click** on as many more files as you want to select. Each will be highlighted.

If you mistakenly click on a file you don't want, continue to hold the Ctrl key and click on the file again. the highlight bar will disappear.

# COPYING FILES WITH DRAG AND DROP

In this section you will copy files in the WINWRITE directory (which you created in Chapter 7, "Customizing Startups") onto a floppy disk in drive A.

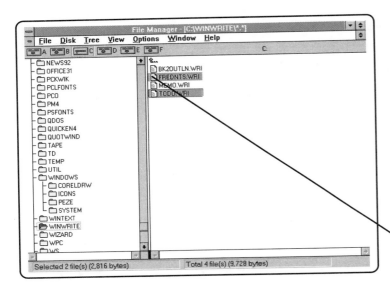

1. **Click** on the **WINWRITE** directory on the left side of the File Manager window. The right side of the File Manager window will display the files in that directory.

2. **Select** the **files** you want to copy. In this example, there are two files.

3. **Place** the **mouse arrow** on the **first highlighted file icon**.

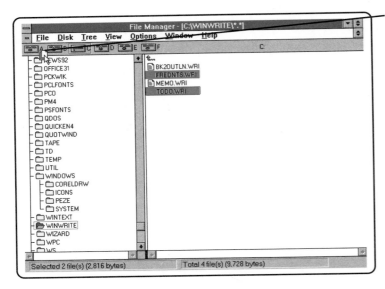

4. **Press and hold** the mouse button as you **drag** the icon to the *destination drive* (the drive to which you want to copy the file; drive A in this example). You will see multiple icons move across the screen. When you **release** the mouse button the Confirm Mouse Operation dialog box will appear.

(Make sure you have a floppy disk in drive A.)

5. **Click** on **Yes**. You will see a message box saying the files are being copied. If a filename already exists on the disk in drive A, you will be asked if you want to replace the file with the new file. Click on Yes if you do. Click on Cancel if you do not want to replace the file.

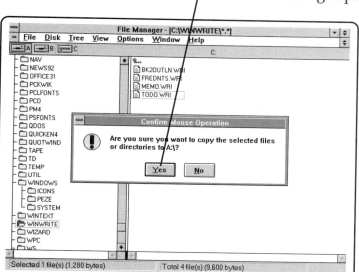

You can also copy files with the File command in the menu bar but it's not nearly as much fun or as fast.

You can check drive A to make sure the files were copied.

6. **Click** on the **A drive icon**.

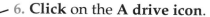

The files on the floppy in drive A will show on the right side of the File Manager window.

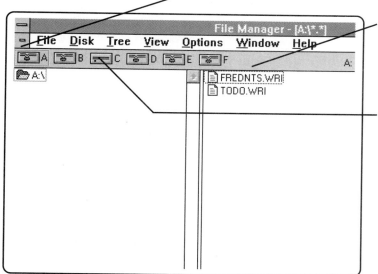

7. **Click** on the **C drive icon** to return to the drive C directory tree.

# MOVING FILES WITH DRAG AND DROP

In this section you will move a file from the WINWRITE directory to the WINTEXT directory on drive C.

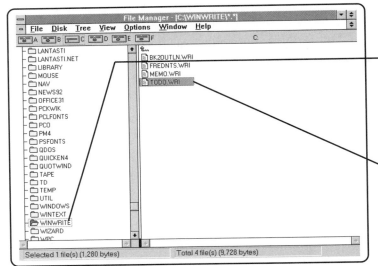

1. **Click** on the **directory** where the file you want to move is located. In this example, it is the WINWRITE directory.

2. **Click** on the **file** you want to move.

3. **Place** the **mouse arrow** on the **file icon**.

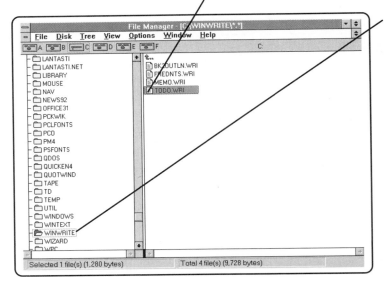

4. **Press and hold** the **Alt** key. At the same time **press** and **hold** the **mouse button** as you **drag** the file icon to the *destination directory* (the directory to which you want to move the file) on the left side of the File Manager window. **Place** the **file icon** over the **directory name**. **Release** the **Alt** key and the **mouse button**. The Confirm Mouse Operation dialog box will appear.

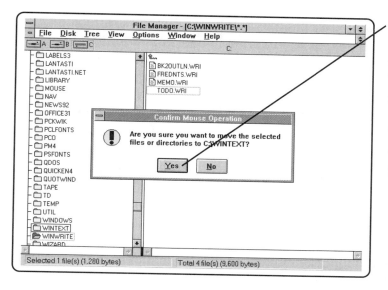

**5. Click** on **Yes** to confirm that you want to move the file. The dialog box will disappear and the file will be moved.

You can also move files with the File command in the menu bar.

# DELETING FILES

**1. Click** on the **directory** that holds the files to be deleted. The files in that directory will be shown on the right side of the File Manager window.

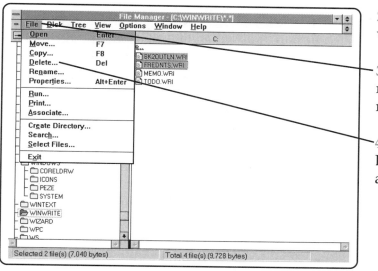

**2. Select** the **file(s)** you want to delete.

**3. Click** on **File** in the menu bar. A pull-down menu will appear.

**4. Click** on **Delete**. The Delete dialog box will appear.

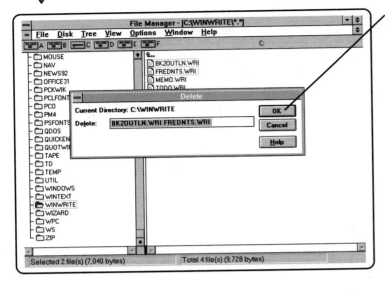

5. **Click** on **OK** to confirm that you want to delete the file(s). The Confirm File Delete dialog box will appear. When you delete a file, it is permanently erased from your disk. Therefore, Windows gives you several opportunities to confirm that you do indeed want to delete the file(s).

6. **Click** on **Yes to All** to erase all the selected files.

If you click on Yes, you will be asked to confirm that you want to erase each individual file that you selected.

If you click on No or Cancel, the delete process will be canceled.

This overview of File Manager covers basic housekeeping procedures. Explore the pull-down menus to discover other functions you can perform.

7. **Close File Manager** by **clicking twice** on the **Control menu box** on the left of the title bar. Or, click on the Minimize button (t) on the right of the title bar to keep File Manager in icon form at the bottom of your screen.

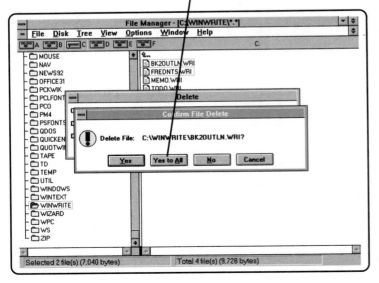

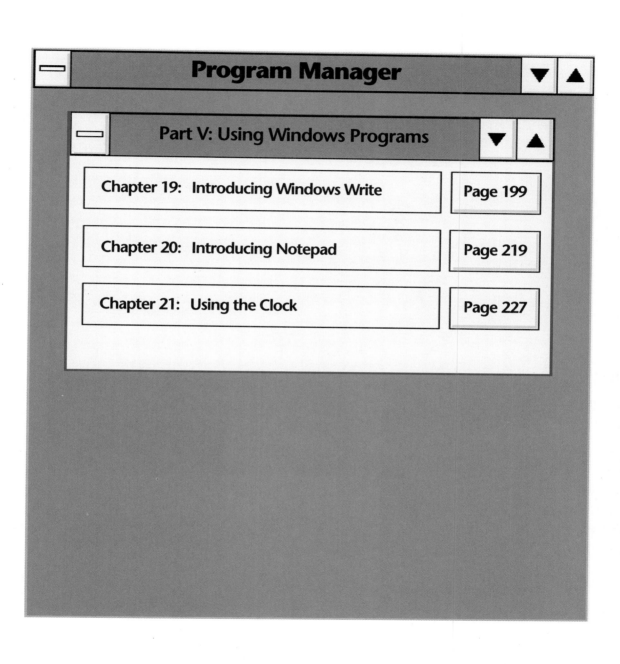

# Program Manager

## Part V: Using Windows Programs

# Introducing Windows Write

Windows Write is a complete word processing program. This chapter will introduce you to the following features in Windows Write:

❖ Opening a document

❖ Setting up margins, tabs, fonts, and print styles

❖ Entering, editing, and moving text

❖ Saving, printing, and closing

## OPENING WINDOWS WRITE

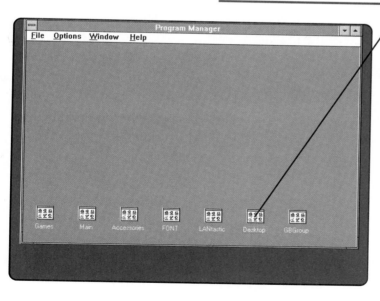

1. **Click twice** on the **group icon** that contains Write. It will be restored to window size. (Write is part of the Accessories group window when you first install Windows. You may have moved it to the Desktop group window in Chapter 5, "Setting Up Your Windows Programs and Groups.")

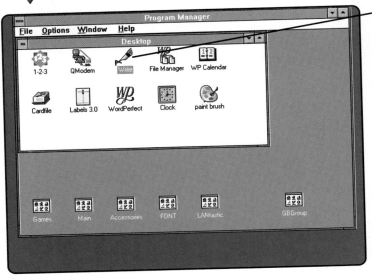

2. **Click twice** on the **Write program icon**. You will see an hourglass. Then an untitled Write document screen will appear.

Notice the flashing *insertion point* at the beginning of the document. This shows where the text will be inserted once you begin typing.

Next to the insertion point is the *end mark*. It marks the end of the text you typed. Both will move as you add text to the page.

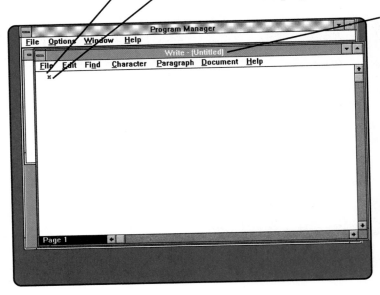

Notice that the Write document is labeled "Untitled." This label will change when you name the document later in this chapter.

Windows Write may appear in a different size and location than the example you see here. Refer to Chapter 1, "Windows' Magical Buttons," and Chapter 2, "Changing the Size and Position of a Window," to enlarge the window or move it.

# SETTING MARGINS

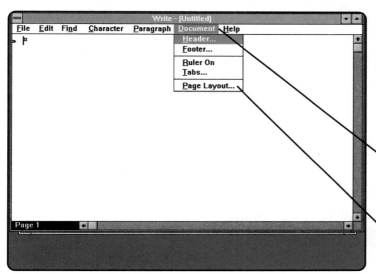

Write is set with margins of 1.25 inches on the left and right and 1 inch at the top and bottom. Each of these can be set individually. In this section you will change the top margin.

1. **Click** on **Document** in the menu bar. A pull-down menu will appear.

2. **Click** on **Page Layout**. The Page Layout dialog box will appear.

3. **Move** the mouse arrow to the **Top Margin text box**. The arrow will change to an I-beam.

4. **Click** to set the cursor in the box.

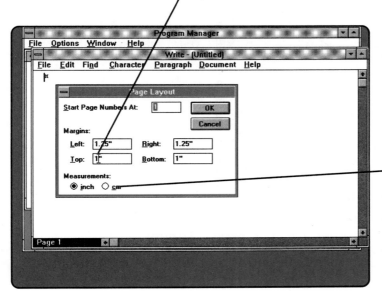

5. **Press and hold** the mouse button as you **drag** the cursor over the **1**. It will be **highlighted**.

6. **Type 1.5** to make the top margin 1.5 inches.

If you want the measurements to be in centimeters, click on cm.

7. **Click** on **OK**. The Page Layout dialog box will close.

# SELECTING A FONT

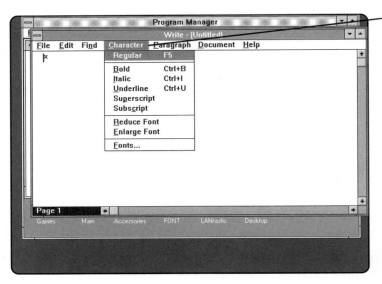

1. **Click** on **Character** in the menu bar. A pull-down menu will appear.

2. **Click** on **Fonts**. The three dots after Fonts (called an ellipsis) indicate that this choice requires additional information. The Font dialog box will appear. It contains a list of the fonts you have installed on Windows.

3. **Click** on the **font** you want for the document. The Sample box will show what the font looks like.

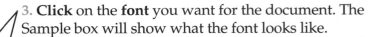

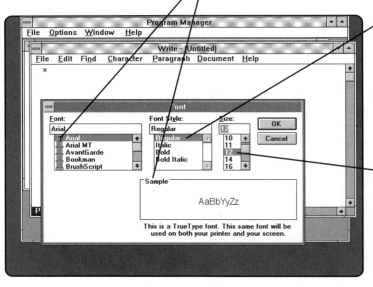

4. **Click** on **Regular** (for regular type) in the Font Style list box. Notice that this font also comes in italic, bold, and bold italic. Some fonts do not offer all these styles.

5. **Click** on **12** in the Size list box. The sample type will increase in size. Type size is measured in points. Text for correspondence and reports is usually 10 to 12 points.

6. **Click** on **OK**. This will set the font, style, and size for the entire document. You can change any or all of these settings to emphasize portions of the text.

# TURNING ON THE RULER LINE

**1. Click** on **Document** in the menu bar. A pull-down menu will appear.

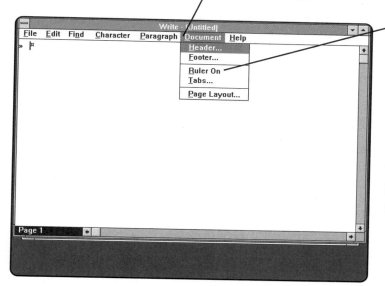

**2. Click** on **Ruler On**. The ruler will appear at the top of the document page. It contains icons that will allow you to set tabs, line spacing, and text alignment at the click of your mouse. Each of these functions can be set through the menu bar, but it is often easier to use the ruler.

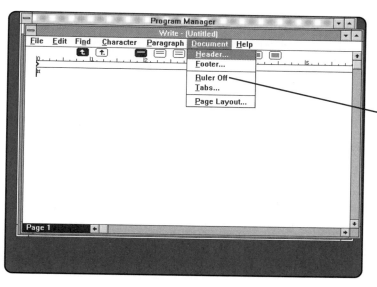

Once the ruler is turned on, the Ruler On option in the Document pull-down menu changes to Ruler Off.

**Click** on **Ruler Off** if you want to take the ruler off your screen.

If you want to follow the procedures in this chapter, keep the ruler turned on.

# SETTING UP LINE SPACING AND TEXT ALIGNMENT

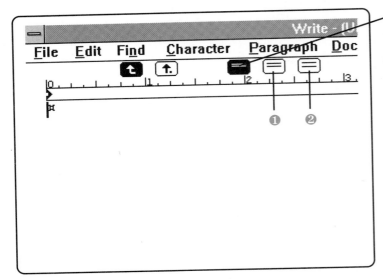

1. **Click** on the **Single Spacing icon** if it is not already highlighted. The other two icons in this group are:

❶ One and One-Half Spacing. This will put a half-line space between typed lines.

❷ Double Spacing. This will put a blank line between typed lines.

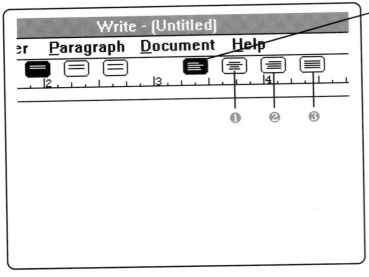

2. **Click** on the **Left Alignment icon** if it is not already highlighted. This will line up all text on the left margin. The other three icons in this group are:

❶ Center Align. This will center each line between the left and right margins.

❷ Right Align. This will line up all text on the right margin.

❸ Justification. This will add extra spaces between words to make all text begin at the left margin and end at the right margin.

# SETTING TABS WITH THE RULER

Write has tabs set every 1/2 inch. In this section you will set a tab at 5/8 inch using the ruler.

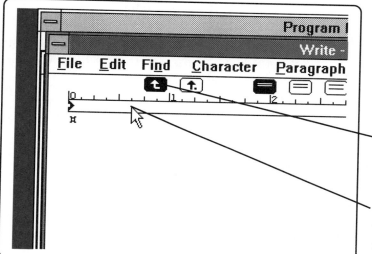

Write has two kinds of tabs each with its own icon. The *text tab* aligns the beginning of words at the tab stop. The *decimal tab* aligns text on periods or decimal points.

**1. Click** on the **Text Tab icon** if it is not already highlighted.

**2. Move** the **mouse arrow** to the space just below the 5/8 inch mark.

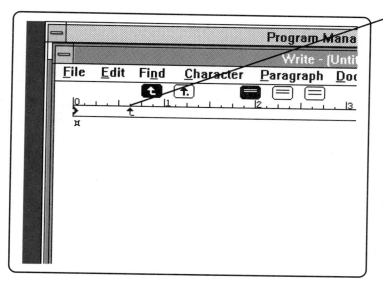

**3. Click** to **set the tab.** A curved arrow text tab will appear in the ruler line at 5/8 inch. When you set a custom tab, it erases the tabs between the left margin and the custom tab.

In the next section, you will use a different method to set a second tab.

# SETTING A TAB WITH THE DOCUMENT COMMAND

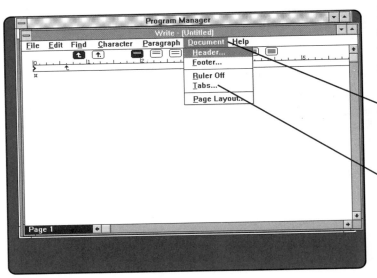

In this section you will set a second tab at 3 inches using the Document option in the menu bar.

1. **Click** on **Document** in the menu bar. A pull-down menu will appear.

2. **Click** on **Tabs**. The Tabs dialog box will appear.

Notice that the tab you set using the ruler is recorded in the Tabs dialog box.

3. **Click** on the **second tab box** to set the cursor. On your screen it will be empty.

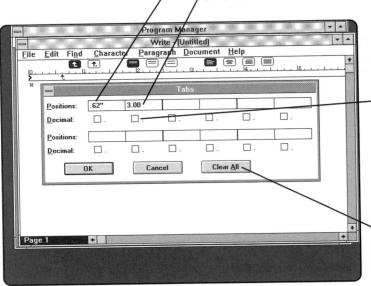

4. **Type 3.00** to set a tab at 3 inches.

If you want the tab to be a decimal tab, click on the Decimal box below the tab position.

5. **Click** on **OK**.

You can clear all tabs by clicking on Clear All then clicking on OK.

# TYPING TEXT IN A NEW DOCUMENT

Now that you have set up the page layout, chosen the font, and set tabs, you are ready to begin typing. Like all word processing programs, Write has a *word wrap* feature. This means you can continue to type without worrying about your right margin. Write will bring the text around to the next line automatically.

Press Enter only at the end of a paragraph. Press Enter twice to double space between paragraphs. In word processing, a paragraph is considered to be any text that is followed by the Enter command. Therefore, the word "MEMO" at the top of this document is considered a paragraph. Press the Enter key twice after "MEMO" and after each of the lines in the heading.

**Type** the **text** you see in the example. It contains an error you will correct later in the chapter, so include it if you want to follow along with these procedures. If you make an unintentional typing error, simply backspace and type the correct letters. Type the current date in place of "Today's Date."

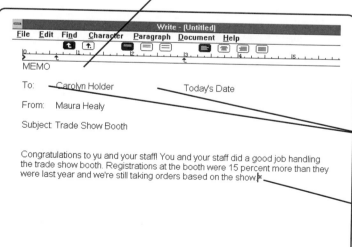

Press the Tab key to insert a tab at the appropriate spots in the memo heading.

Notice the insertion point and the end mark move as you type.

# EDITING TEXT

This section will cover basic editing procedures. These procedures apply to all Windows programs.

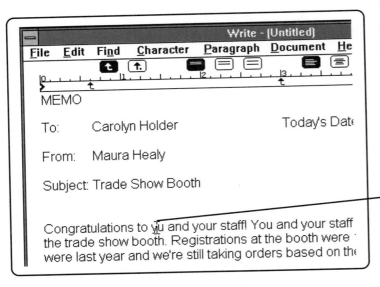

## Inserting Text

When you are in the typing area of the screen the mouse arrow appears as an I-beam.

1. **Place the** I-beam **between** the letters **y** and **u**.

2. **Click** to set the cursor in place.

3. **Type** the letter **o**. It will be inserted into the space. You can insert letters, words, or entire paragraphs this way.

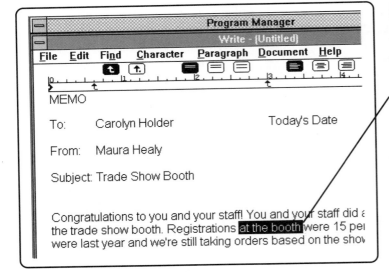

## Deleting Text

1. **Click** at the **beginning of the text** you want to delete.

2. **Press and hold** the mouse button as you **drag** the **highlight bar** over the words and space to be deleted. **Release** the mouse button.

3. **Press** the **Del** key to delete the text.

# Replacing Text

In this section you will highlight the word you want to change and replace it with another word.

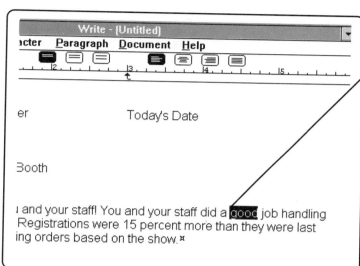

1. **Click** at the **beginning of** the word **good**.

2. **Press and hold** the mouse button as you **drag** the **highlight bar** over the word. **Release** the mouse button.

3. **Type** the word **terrific**. It will replace the highlighted material.

# MOVING TEXT

In this section you will cut a piece of text from one part of the memo and paste it into another part.

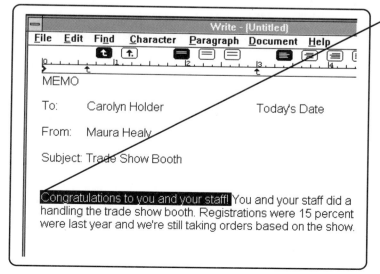

1. **Move** the I-beam to the **beginning of Congratulations**.

2. **Click** to set the insertion point in place.

3. **Press and hold** the mouse button as you **drag** the **highlight bar** across the entire sentence and the space after it. Release the mouse button.

4. **Click** on **Edit** in the menu bar. A pull-down menu will appear.

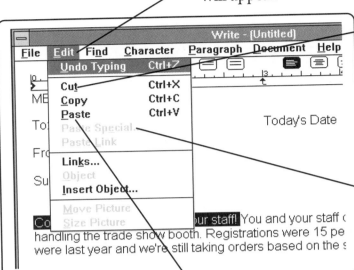

5. **Click** on **Cut**. The highlighted text will disappear. It is sent to the Clipboard, where it will stay until you paste it somewhere or replace it in Clipboard with other material.

Notice that some of the choices on the pull-down menu are in light gray. This means they are not currently available.

If you cut or copied in any Windows program prior to this procedure, there is data in your Clipboard. This means the Paste option is available and will be in dark type.

You will now place the selected text as a separate line at the end of the memo.

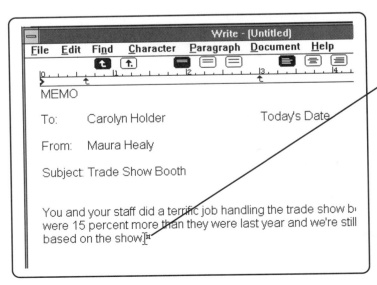

6. **Click** to set the insertion point at the end of the typed material, just after the period and before the end mark.

7. **Press Enter twice** to insert a blank line after the end of the memo. The insertion point and end mark will move.

**8. Click** on **Edit** in the menu bar. A pull-down menu will appear.

**9. Click** on **Paste**. The text you cut will be pasted in the document at the insertion point.

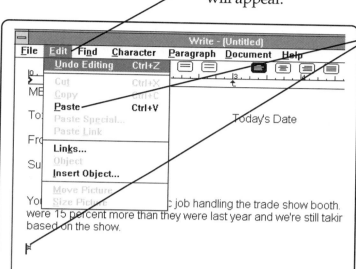

# CENTERING TEXT

In this section you will center the line "Congratulations to you and your staff!"

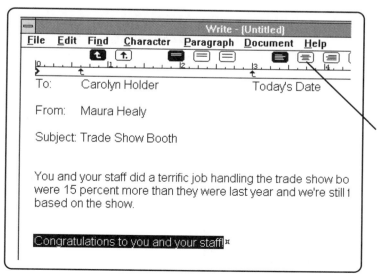

**1. Highlight** the **sentence** by clicking at the beginning (or end) of the sentence and **dragging** the **highlight bar** across the sentence.

**2. Click** on the **Center Align** icon in the ruler. The highlighted text will be centered.

# CHANGING TYPE STYLE TO BOLD

In this section you will change the type style of a sentence to make it bold so it stands out. Normally, you first highlight the text you want to make bold. If you are following these procedures, you already highlighted the "Congratulations..." sentence at the end of the memo.

1. **Click** on **Character** in the menu bar. A pull-down menu will appear.

2. **Click** on **Bold**. The highlighted text will appear in bold.

# NAMING AND SAVING THE DOCUMENT

1. **Click** on **File** in the menu bar. A pull-down menu will appear.

2. **Click** on **Save As**. The Save As dialog box will appear.

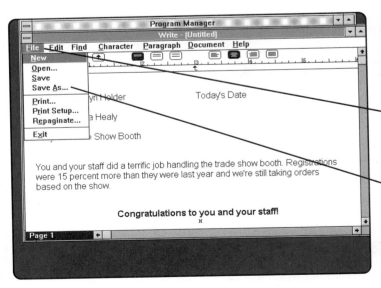

**3.** Since the cursor is already flashing in the File Name text box, **type** a **name** for the file. A filename can have up to eight letters. Do not use spaces, periods, or commas in the name.

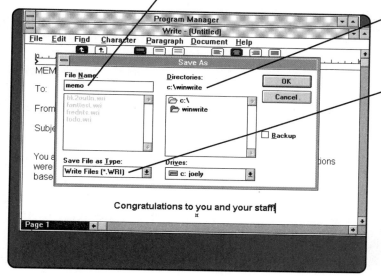

Notice that the file will be stored in the C:\WINWRITE directory.

The extension will be .WRI. The Write program will add this extension automatically.

**4. Click** on **OK** in the upper-right corner of the dialog box. The dialog box will disappear and the name (MEMO.WRI) will appear in the title bar of the document.

# CLOSING A FILE

Normally you save a file before you close it. If you have been following these procedures, you saved and named the document with the Save As command.

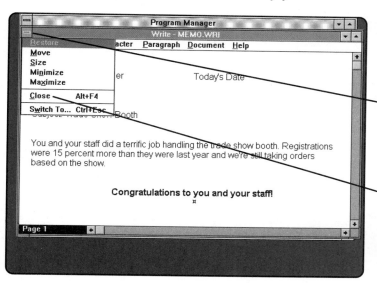

**1. Click** on the **Control menu box** on the left of the Write title bar. A pull-down menu will appear.

**2. Click** on **Close**. Write will close and the customized Desktop (or Accessories) group window will be on your screen.

# OPENING A SAVED FILE

In this section you will open the memo you created and edit it.

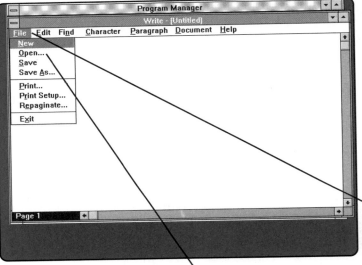

1. **Click twice** on the **Write icon** in the Desktop (or Accessories) group window.

An untitled Write document will be on your screen. (See "Opening Windows Write" at the beginning of this chapter if you need help.)

2. **Click** on **File** in the menu bar. A pull-down menu will appear.

3. **Click** on **Open**. The Open dialog box will appear.

4. **Click** on the **filename** you gave to the memo. Use the down arrow on the scroll bar to scroll through the list, if necessary.

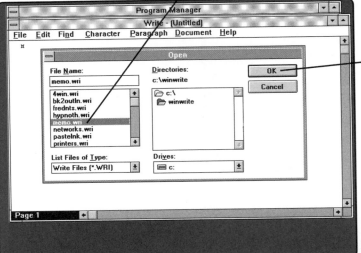

5. **Click** on **OK**. The file will appear on your screen.

# ADDING TEXT
# TO A SAVED FILE

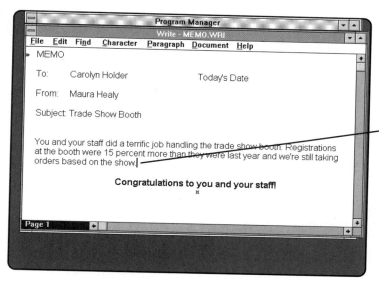

Once a file is open, you can follow standard editing procedures. In this section you will add a sentence to the memo.

**1. Click** at the **end of the first paragraph** to set the insertion point.

**2. Press Enter twice** to double space.

**3. Type** the sentence **Let's start planning for the next show**.

# PRINTING

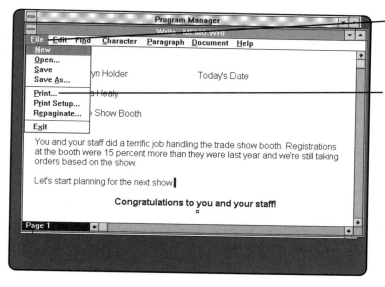

**1. Click** on **File** in the menu bar. A pull-down menu will appear.

**2. Click** on **Print**. The Print dialog box will appear.

3. **Click** on **All** if it is not already selected. This will print the entire document.

You can print selected pages of a long document by clicking on Pages, then typing the page numbers you want to print.

See Chapter 13, "Basic Printer Settings," and Chapter 15, "Special Printing Options," for discussions of the other elements in the Print dialog box.

4. **Click** on **OK**. The Print dialog box will disappear and a message box will appear briefly, stating, "Now printing MEMO.WRI." The document will print unless you click on Cancel in the message box.

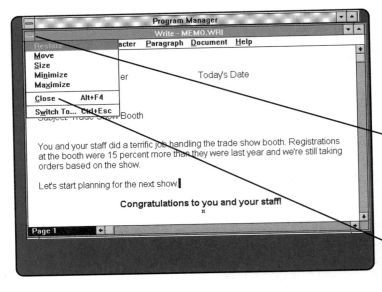

# CLOSING— WITH OR WITHOUT SAVING

1. **Click** on the **Control menu box** on the left of the MEMO.WRI title bar. A pull-down menu will appear.

2. **Click** on **Close**. Since you did not save the changes you made above, the Write dialog box will appear.

3. **Click** on **Yes**. MEMO.WRI will be saved with the changes you just made. Write will disappear and you will be back to the customized Desktop (or Accessories) group window.

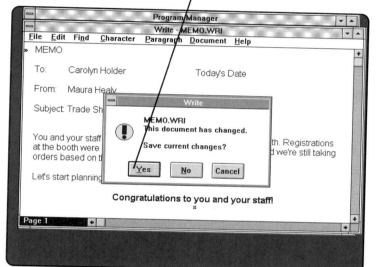

If you click on No, the file will close but the changes will not be saved. The MEMO.WRI file will revert to what it was before you made any changes.

If you click on Cancel, the Write dialog box will disappear and the memo will be on your screen. The Close command will be canceled.

Windows Write has many more features. This introduction was designed to give you the confidence to experiment with features such as page breaks, find, replace, inserting pictures, and making backup copies of files. Many of the functions you performed in this chapter are applicable to other more powerful Windows-based word processing programs such as Word for Windows, WordPerfect for Windows, and WordStar for Windows. Write files are fully transferable to Word for Windows and many other Windows-based word processing programs.

# Introducing Notepad

Just like a notepad on your desk, Windows Notepad is a handy way to make notes to yourself and to compile a To Do list. Notepad also allows you to log the date and time so it is an ideal way to keep track of billable (or other) hours. Notepad saves files in an ASCII (pronounced "as key") format, which is an almost universally recognized text format. This allows you to transfer Notepad files to almost any word processing program. In this introduction to Notepad you will:

❖ Open a Notepad file

❖ Log in the date and time

❖ Save and print a file

## OPENING NOTEPAD

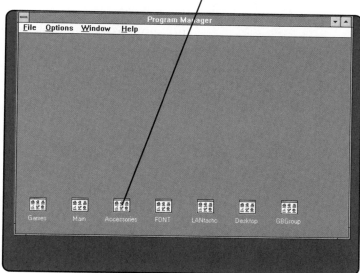

**1. Click twice** on the **Accessories group icon** (or the customized Desktop group icon) at the bottom of your screen. It will be restored to window size. If you have been following the procedures in this book you may have moved Notepad to the Desktop group window.

2. **Click twice** on the **Notepad icon**. It may be in a different spot in your group window. An untitled Notepad screen will appear.

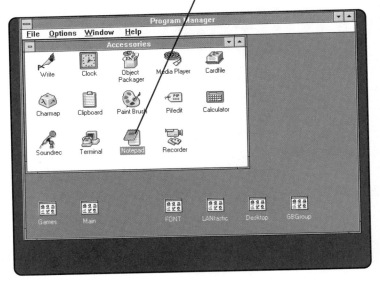

Notepad may appear in a different size and a different place on your screen. See Chapter 1, "Windows' Magical Buttons," and Chapter 2, "Changing the Size and Position of a Window," to move or resize the Notepad window.

This Notepad file will remain untitled until you name it later in this chapter.

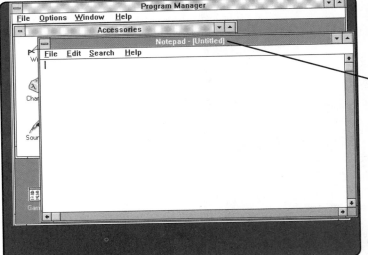

# CREATING A TIME LOG: METHOD #1

If you need to keep track of your time, you will like Notepad's Time/Date feature. Method #1 adds a time/date notation every time you select the Time/Date command in the Edit pull-down menu.

Use this method if you like to keep Notepad running in icon form at the bottom of your screen, or in a tile or cascade setup.

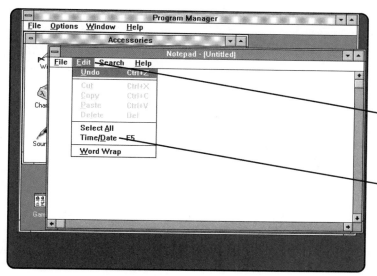

**1. Click** on **Edit** in the menu bar. A pull-down menu will appear.

**2. Click** on **Time/Date**. Notepad will insert the time and date in the file. Do this when you start working on a project.

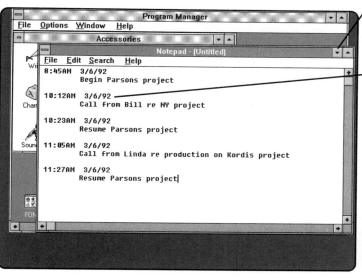

**3. Click** on the **Minimize button** (▼) to reduce Notepad to its icon form.

If you get interrupted with phone calls or work related to other projects, click twice on the Notepad icon to bring it up on your screen. Log in the start and stop times of the phone calls or other work with the Time/Date option. This allows you to keep an accurate record of time spent on each project.

# CREATING A TIME LOG: METHOD #2

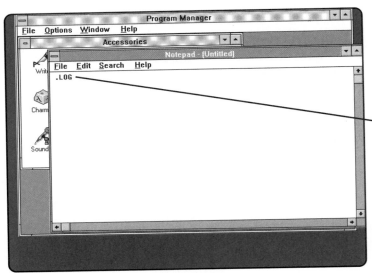

The second method of creating a time log works only if you open and close Notepad each time you use it.

**1. Type .LOG in capital letters** in the first line at the left margin. This does not create a time/date notation yet. It will add the notation to the end of the file each time you open the Notepad file.

With this method you need to save and name the file, close it, then open it when you want to make another note. See the sections on "Saving and Naming a Notepad File" later in this chapter and "Opening a Saved File" in Chapter 19.

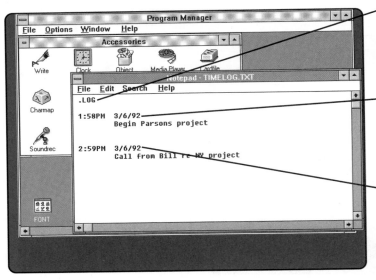

In this example you saved and closed the file after you typed in .LOG at the top left margin.

When you opened the file the time and date were inserted. You made a note to yourself and closed the file.

When you opened the file to insert another note about a phone call, Notepad inserted the time and date again.

# WORD WRAPPING

Since Notepad is a simple word processing program, it does not wrap text automatically to the next line. The text will go beyond the right border of the window unless you turn on the Word Wrap option.

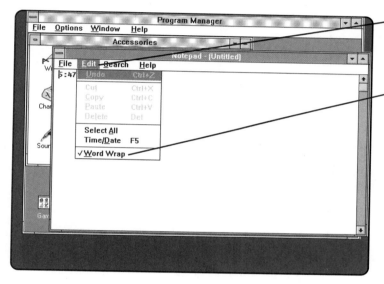

1. **Click** on **Edit** in the menu bar. A pull-down menu will appear.

2. **Click** on **Word Wrap**. The menu will close. Text will now wrap automatically to the next line. (Click on Word Wrap again to turn it off.)

In Notepad you control the length of the text line by controlling the size of the window. (See Chapter 2, "Changing the Size and Position of a Window," if you need help.) If you enlarge the window, the text line will be long. If you decrease the size of the window, the text line will be short.

The line breaks created by word wrap will not be transferred if you paste the text into another program. The text will conform to the page setup of the new program into which you paste it.

# INSERTING TEXT AND EDITING

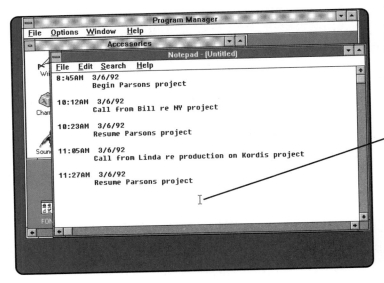

You type and edit text in Notepad the same way you do in Write. (See Chapter 19, "Introducing Windows Write," for detailed directions.)

The mouse arrow becomes an I-beam within the typing area. Use it just as you do in Write.

Notepad has tabs set every half inch. You cannot change these settings.

# SAVING AND NAMING A NOTEPAD FILE

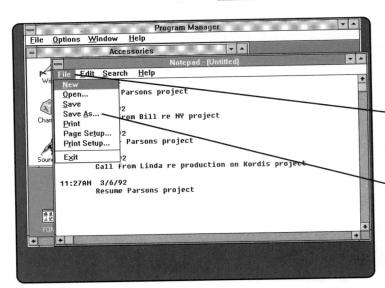

Saving and naming a Notepad file is the same process you use in Windows Write.

1. **Click** on **File** in the menu bar. A pull-down menu will appear.

2. **Click** on **Save As**. The Save As dialog box will appear.

**3. Type** a **name** of up to eight characters for the file. Don't use punctuation marks or spaces. Refer to the Windows documentation for more

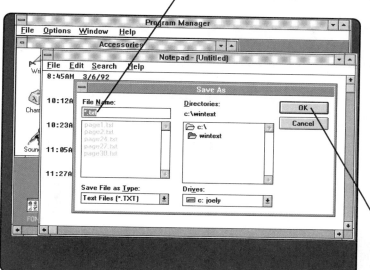

details on filenames. Since the File Name text box is already highlighted, you can just begin typing. The name you type will replace "*.txt."

Windows automatically adds the .TXT extension to all Notepad files.

**4. Click** on **OK**. The name you typed will appear in the title bar of the Notepad file.

# CHANGING THE PAGE SETUP

Notepad files print with standard margins plus the filename and a page number. These can be changed.

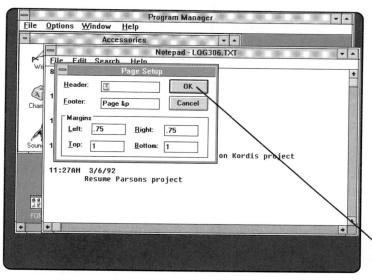

**1. Click** on **File** in the menu bar. A pull-down menu will appear.

**2. Click** on **Page Setup**. The Page Setup dialog box will appear.

Any of these settings can be changed by clicking in the text box and typing the new setting.

**3. Click** on **OK** to confirm changes, or on Cancel to close without changes.

# PRINTING AND CLOSING THE NOTEPAD

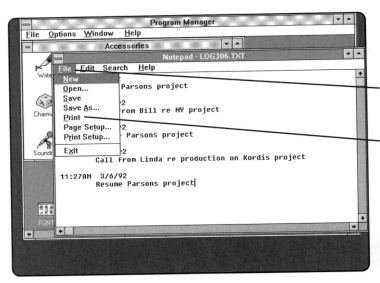

Printing procedures are the same in all Windows-based programs.

**1. Click** on **File** in the menu bar.

**2. Click** on **Print** in the pull-down menu. The file will be sent to the printer.

Closing a Notepad file also follows the Windows standard procedure.

**3. Click** on the **Control menu box** on the left of the Notepad title bar. A pull-down menu will appear.

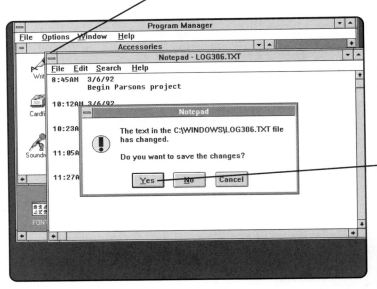

**4. Click** on **Close**. If you saved the file before you clicked on Close, Notepad will simply close. If you did not save the file the Notepad dialog box will appear.

**5. Click** on **Yes** to save changes. The file will close.

To open a saved Notepad file, see "Opening a Saved File" in Chapter 19. The steps are the same.

# Using the Clock

The Clock is an important feature of Windows. Not only is it helpful to have the time and date on your screen, but the Clock is also used by other Windows programs. File Manager records the date and time on files and Calendar, of course, is totally dependent on the Clock. In this chapter you will:

❖ Set the time and date

❖ Change to international settings if you choose

❖ Set the Clock to run in analog or digital mode

❖ Set the Clock to be on your screen at all times in a minimized form

## SETTING THE TIME AND DATE

Time and date are set through the Control Panel in the Main group window.

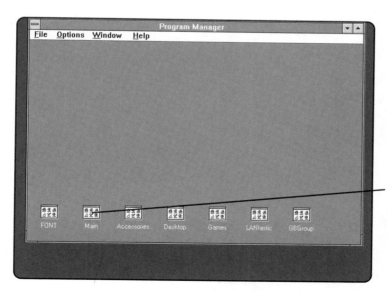

The icons shown in this chapter may appear in different positions in your windows. The windows and dialog boxes may appear in different sizes and positions than shown here. That's okay.

1. **Click twice** on the **Main group icon**. The Main group window will appear.

2. **Click twice** on the **Control Panel icon**. The Control Panel window will appear.

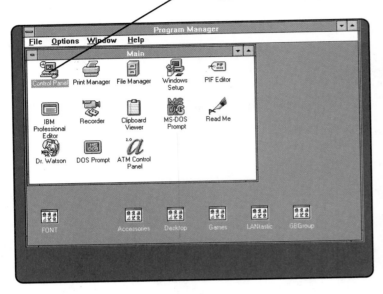

3. **Click twice** on the **Date/Time icon**. The Date & Time dialog box will appear.

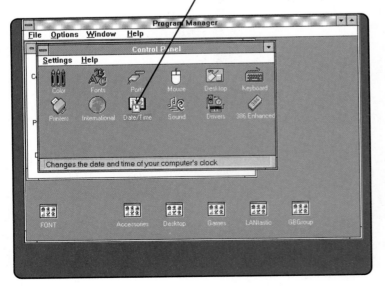

There are two way to change the date and time on the Clock. Both ways require you to highlight or select the number you want to change. This section will show you two ways to change the day. You can follow the same procedure to change the rest of the date and the time.

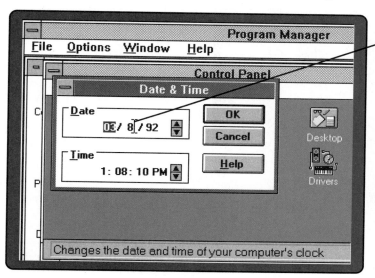

4. **Move** the **mouse arrow beside** the number **8**. The arrow will change to an I-beam.

5. **Click** to set it in place. It will change to a flashing bar.

6. **Press and hold** the mouse button as you **drag** the **highlight bar** over the number. Then use Method #1 or #2 to change the number.

# Method #1

7a. **Type** a **new number**. It will replace the highlighted number.

# Method #2

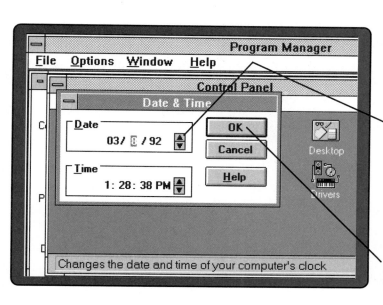

7b. **Click** on the **up arrow** to increase the number, or, on the **down arrow** to decrease the number.

Follow these procedures to change other numbers.

8. **Click** on **OK** to save the changes.

# SETTING INTERNATIONAL TIME

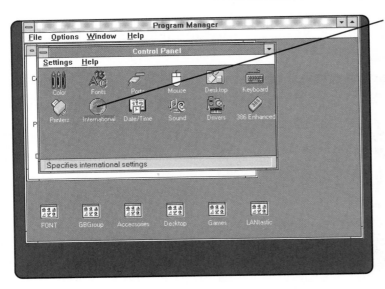

1. **Click twice** on the **International icon** in the Control Panel group window. The International dialog box will appear.

Notice that in addition to the time and date, you can change the settings for Country, Language, Keyboard Layout, Measurement, List Separator, Currency Format, and Number Format.

2. **Click** on **Change** in the Time Format box. The International Time Format dialog box will appear.

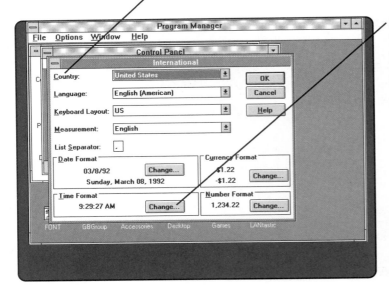

3. **Click** on the appropriate **circles** for the options you prefer.

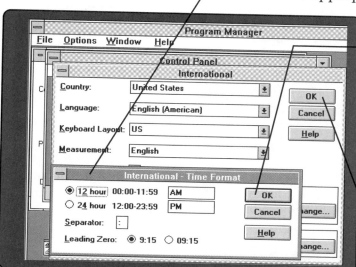

4. **Click** on **OK** to confirm the changes. Or click on Cancel to close the box without making changes. The International - Time Format dialog box will disappear. The International dialog box will be on your screen.

5. **Click** on **OK** in the International dialog box to confirm the changes (or, click on Cancel). The dialog box will disappear and the Control Panel window will appear. The date can be changed by clicking on Change in the Date Format box. See the Windows 3.1 documentation for more details.

6. **Click** on the **Control menu box** on the left of the Control Panel title bar. A pull-down menu will appear.

7. **Click** on **Close**. The Control Panel will disappear and the Main group window will be on your screen.

8. **Click** on the **Minimize button** (▼) in the right corner of the Main group window title bar. The Main group window will be minimized to an icon at the bottom of your screen.

# SETTING THE CLOCK

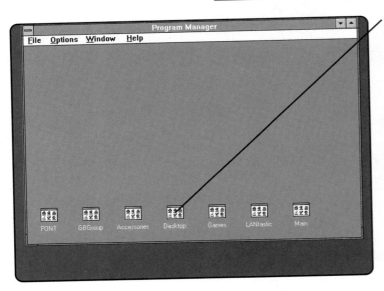

1. **Click twice** on the **group icon** that contains the Clock. When you first install Windows the Clock is in the Accessories group window. You may have moved it to your customized Desktop group window. In this example, the Desktop group window will appear.

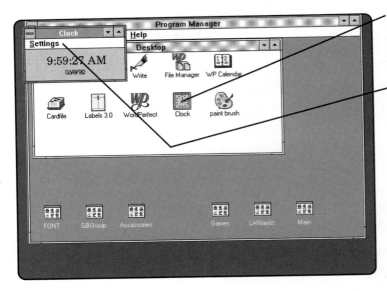

2. **Click twice** on the **Clock icon**. The Clock menu will appear.

3. **Click** on **Settings**. A pull-down menu will appear.

4. **Click** on the **settings** you want for your Clock. The pull-down menu will close after each click. If you want to change more than one setting, click on Settings to pull down the menu for each change.

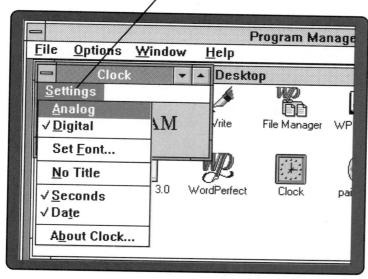

❖ Analog will display a round Clock with ticking hands. Digital will display the time in numbers.

❖ Set Font will bring up the Font dialog box in which you can choose the font for the Clock.

❖ No Title will make the title bar disappear. To restore the title bar, click twice on the Clock dialog box.

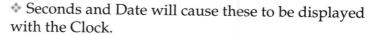

❖ Seconds and Date will cause these to be displayed with the Clock.

❖ About Clock will display how much memory you have left in your system and how much of your system resources are free.

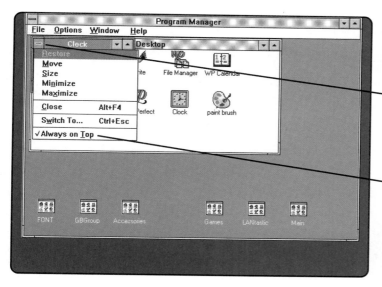

5. **Click** on the **Control menu box** on the left of the Clock title bar. A pull-down menu will appear.

6. **Click** on **Always on Top** to ensure that the Clock will be visible on your desktop and not get hidden behind other Windows programs.

# SETTING THE CLOCK TO RUN MINIMIZED

In this section you will set the Clock to run in a minimized version at the bottom of your screen.

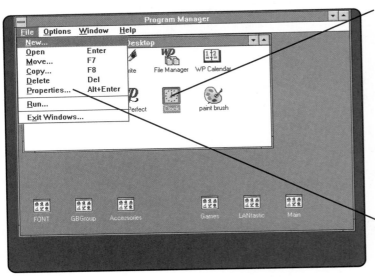

1. **Click once** on the **Clock icon** in your Desktop (or Accessories) group window. The name below the Clock face will be highlighted.

2. **Click** on **File** in the Program Manager menu bar. A pull-down menu will appear.

3. **Click** on **Properties**. The Program Item Properties dialog box will appear.

4. **Click** on **Run Minimized** to insert an X in the box. Now when you click twice on the Clock icon, it will immediately go to an icon at the bottom of your screen.

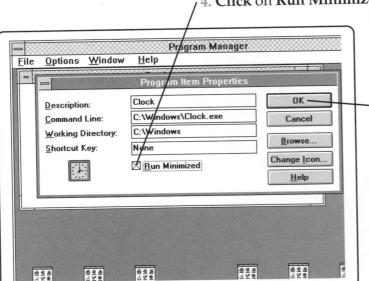

5. **Click** on **OK** to close the dialog box.

6. **Click** on the **Minimize button (▼)** in the Desktop title bar to close it.

To move the Clock any place on your screen, see Chapter 2, "Changing the Size and Position of a Window."

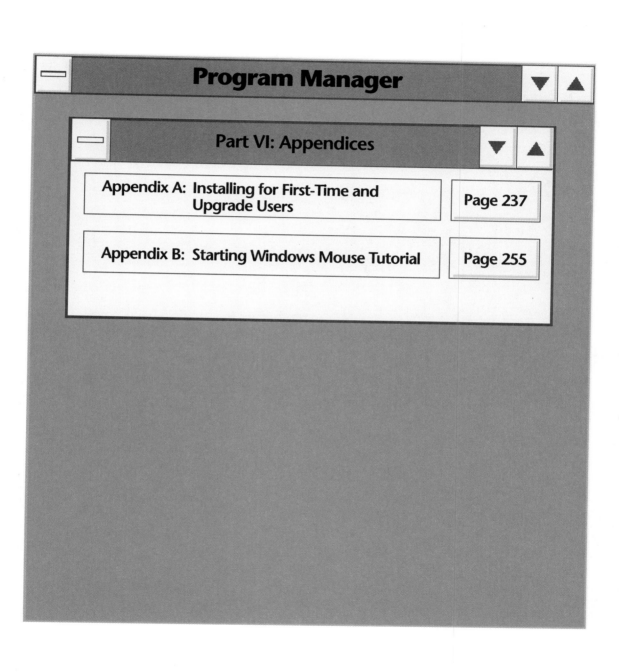

**Program Manager**

**Part VI: Appendices**

# Installing for First-Time and Upgrade Users

If you are a new user, begin your Windows 3.1 installation on page 240. If you are upgrading from a previous version, begin your installation on this page.

In this appendix you will:

❖ Back up critical files and disks

❖ Install Windows 3.1 for the first time or as an upgrade

## UPGRADE USERS START HERE

If you are upgrading to Windows 3.1, you may have customized your previous version. You may have installed programs such as Word for Windows and special font packages or created special group windows. Backing up these critical files is the only way to make certain your customized features are available to you after you upgrade. There are three kinds of critical files, along with some special program files, to be backed up:

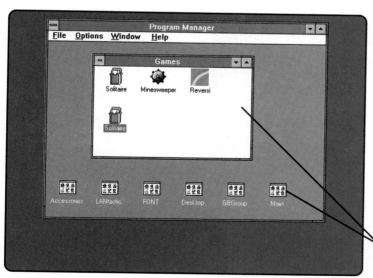

❖ **Files that end with the extension .GRP.**

These files manage your group windows and icons.

**237**

❖ **Files that end with the extension .PIF**. These files make your DOS programs work in Windows. For example, the PIF file that makes WordStar 6.0 for DOS work in Windows is called WS.PIF.

The program icons in the top row of this window run DOS programs. They are controlled by PIF files.

❖ **Files that end with the extension .INI**. These files tell Windows how it is set up and how to relate to other programs.

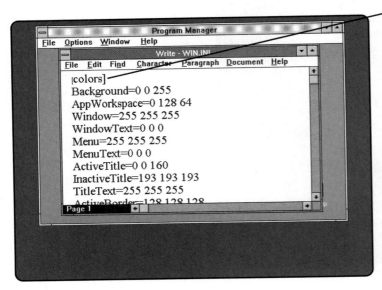

In this example you see a cropped section of a WIN.INI file. It is labeled [colors] and contains the information that tells Windows what colors you have selected for the screen elements. If you should accidentally lose your WIN.INI file in the upgrade installation, you will have to start from scratch if you want to set up Windows to look the same as it was before the upgrade.

# BACKING UP CRITICAL WINDOWS FILES BEFORE UPGRADING

1. **Insert** a new, formatted disk in drive A (or drive B).

2. At the DOS prompt (C:\>), **type cd/windows** and **press Enter**. The WINDOWS directory prompt will appear.

```
C:\>cd\windows
C:\WINDOWS>copy *.grp a:
DESKTOP.GRP
ADLUS.GRP
LANTASTI.GRP
        3 file(s) copied

C:\WINDOWS>copy *.pif a:
QDOS3.PIF
WS.PIF
        3 file(s) copied
```

3. At the Windows prompt (C:\WINDOWS>), **type copy *.grp a:** (there is a space after "copy" and after ".grp") and **press Enter**. A list of the files with the extension .GRP will be shown as they are copied. When the copying is finished, the Windows prompt will reappear.

4. At the Windows prompt, **type copy *.pif a:** and **press Enter**. A list of the files with the extension .PIF will be shown as they are copied.

```
C:\WINDOWS>copy *.ini a:
123.INI
ATM.INI
COLLAGE.INI
        3 files(s) copied

C:\WINDOWS> copy collage.exe a:
        1 file(s) copied

C:\WINDOWS > copy atmcntrl.exe a:
        1 file(s) copied
```

5. At the Windows prompt **type copy *.ini a:** and **press Enter**. Files with the extension .INI will be copied.

6. **Repeat** the process for important files from other programs. In this example the ATMCNTRL.EXE file from Adobe Type Manager and COLLAGE.EXE file from Collage Plus files are backed up because they run programs through the Windows directory.

# NEW AND UPGRADE USERS: BACK UP YOUR CRITICAL DOS FILES

When you install Windows 3.1 for the first time or as an upgrade, it changes your AUTOEXEC.BAT and the CONFIG.SYS files. These two critical files determine how your computer works. In case something goes wrong, you need to back up these two files.

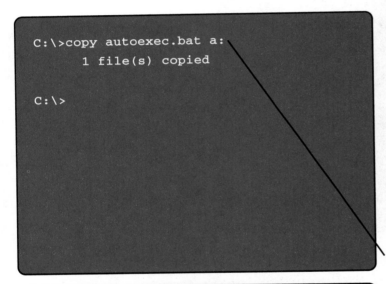

```
C:\>copy autoexec.bat a:
       1 file(s) copied

C:\>
```

**1. Insert** a new, formatted disk into drive A. If you are upgrading, use a different disk from the one you used to back up your critical Windows files in the previous section.

**2.** At the DOS prompt (C:\>), **type copy autoexec.bat a:** and **press Enter**. There is a space after "copy" and after ".bat". You will get a message when the file is copied to the disk in drive A.

```
C:\>copy autoexec.bat a:
       1 file(s) copied

C:\>copy config.sys a:
       1 file(s) copied

C:\>
```

**3.** At the DOS prompt (C:\>), **type: copy config.sys a:** and **press Enter**. There is a space after "copy" and after ".sys". You will get a message when the file is copied to the disk in drive A.

# NEW AND UPGRADE USERS: BACK UP YOUR WINDOWS 3.1 DISKS!

```
C:\>diskcopy a: a:

Insert SOURCE diskette in drive A:

Press any key to continue...

Copying 88 tracks
18 sectors per track, 2 sides(s)

Insert TARGET diskette in drive A:

Press any key to continue...
```

1. **Insert the Windows disk** to be copied in **drive A** (or B). Remember, if you are copying *from* a 1.4MB (megabyte) floppy, you must copy to a 1.4MB floppy. If you try to use the Diskcopy command to copy to a different capacity floppy, DOS will not let you do so.

2. **Type diskcopy a: a:** and **press Enter**. There is a space after "diskcopy" and after the first "a:".

3. **Follow the directions** on your screen. Remember, the *SOURCE* diskette is the Windows 3.1 disk. The *TARGET* diskette is the blank formatted disk. It takes a number of passes to copy a disk completely. Continue to insert the same SOURCE disk and the same TARGET disk until you are asked if you want to copy another diskette. Then begin the process again with the second Windows disk and a second blank TARGET disk and so on until all the disks are copied.

```
Insert SOURCE diskette in drive A:
Press any key to continue...
Insert TARGET diskette in drive A:
Press any key to continue...
Insert SOURCE diskette in drive A:
Press any key to continue...
Insert TARGET diskette in drive A:
Press any key to continue...
Volume Serial Number is 22DG-1J1B
Copy another diskette (Y/N)?
```

# INSTALLING WINDOWS 3.1: NEW AND UPGRADE USERS

Windows 3.1 interacts with your system as it installs itself. Depending on whether you are upgrading or are a first-time user, you may or may not see the exact same screens included in the examples in this section. Most of the installation steps, however, are the same whether you are an upgrade- or a first-time user. Simply follow the directions on the screens as they appear.

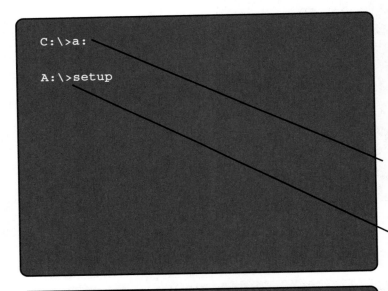

1. **Insert Windows 3.1 Disk #1** in **drive A** (or drive B).

2. **Type a:** (or b:) at the DOS prompt (C:\>) and **press Enter**.

3. **Type setup** at the A:\> (or B:\>) prompt and **press Enter**. There will be a delay before the Windows Setup screen appears. If you are using a non-Windows cache program, you may see a warning screen. Many of the Windows Setup screens give you options. Read each screen and proceed accordingly.

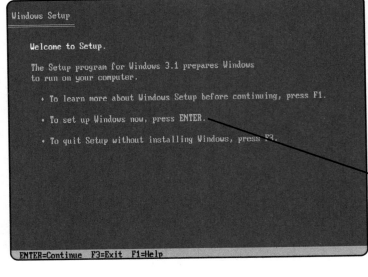

4. **Press Enter** to begin the Windows setup. Or, press the appropriate key for the option you have chosen.

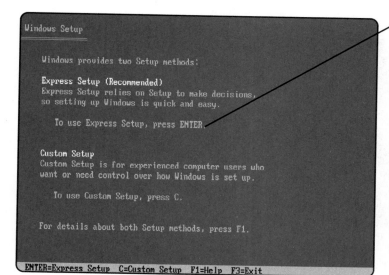

```
Windows Setup

    Windows provides two Setup methods:

    Express Setup (Recommended)
    Express Setup relies on Setup to make decisions,
    so setting up Windows is quick and easy.

        To use Express Setup, press ENTER.


    Custom Setup
    Custom Setup is for experienced computer users who
    want or need control over how Windows is set up.

        To use Custom Setup, press C.


    For details about both Setup methods, press F1.


ENTER=Express Setup   C=Custom Setup   F1=Help   F3=Exit
```

**5. Press Enter** to use the Express Setup. Unless you are very knowledgeable about Windows, Express Setup is the best choice.

If you are installing for the first time, the screens you see in the next several steps will be different. New users please proceed to step 7 on the next page.

```
Windows Setup

    Setup has found a previous version of Microsoft Windows on your hard
    disk in the path shown below.

        • To upgrade this version of Windows to version 3.1, press ENTER.

    If you want to keep the older version of Windows intact and add
    Windows version 3.1 to your system, type a new path in the edit
    box. Use the BACKSPACE key to erase the path shown, and then type the
    new path.

        • When the path is correct, press ENTER to continue.


    C:\WINDOWS

    Note: If you keep both Windows versions on your system, make sure that
    only version 3.1 is listed in the PATH in your AUTOEXEC.BAT file.
    Running older versions of Windows system files can cause problems.


ENTER=Continue   F1=Help   F3=Exit
```

**6. Press Enter** to install Windows 3.1. This procedure will install Windows 3.1 in place of your current version unless you specify a different directory.

```
Windows Setup

   You have told Setup to upgrade your previous version of Windows to
   Windows version 3.1. Please verify this is what you want to do.

      • To have Setup perform an upgrade, press ENTER. (For information
        about the benefits/effects of upgrading, press F1.)

      • To keep your previous version of Windows and add Windows
        version 3.1 to your system (not recommended), press ESC.

   Note: If keeping both versions, PATH in your AUTOEXEC.BAT file should
   list only version 3.1, to avoid running older Windows system files
   with 3.1. Also, any applications already set up for use with Windows
   must be set up again from version 3.1.




   ENTER=Continue   ESC=Cancel   F1=Help
```

**7. Press Enter** to have Setup perform an upgrade or to install Windows for the first time. If you are installing for the first time, your screen may be different.

A message will appear briefly that says, "Please wait while Setup checks your system for configuration information." Another screen with the words "Windows Setup" will appear briefly.

```
Windows Setup

   Please wait while Setup copies files to your hard disk.

      • To quit Setup without installing Windows, press F3.

   For More information on setting up and using Windows 3.1,
   see the "Getting Started" booklet.






      Setup is copying files...
                              5%

      ■


   F3=Exit                              Copying : GDI.EXE
```

This screen shows you the percentage of files being copied. You will hear a beep when approximately 50% of the files have been copied. Another screen will appear and Windows will ask you to insert Disk #2.

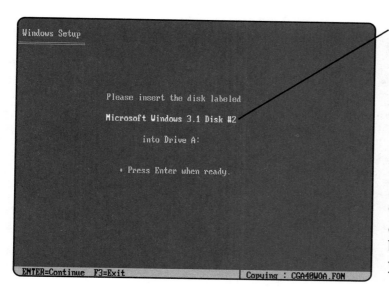

**8. Insert Disk #2** into **drive A** and **press Enter**. If you make a mistake and insert the wrong disk, Windows will stop and ask you to insert the correct disk. The Windows Setup screen will appear again and show the percentage of files being copied. When approximately 90% of the files have been copied, you will hear a beep. Windows will ask you to insert Disk #3.

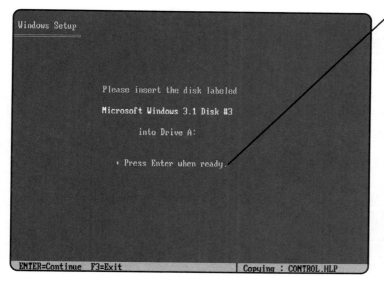

**9. Insert Disk #3** into **drive A** and **press Enter**.

The Windows Setup screen will appear and show the progress of files being copied.

When the rest of the files in this phase have been copied, the screen will go blank. An hourglass will appear briefly.

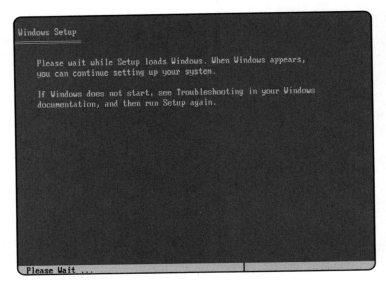

Wait while Setup loads Windows. If Windows does not start or you get an error message, see your user's manual or call Windows Technical Service.

10. **Move** the mouse arrow to the **Name text box**. It will change to an I-beam.

11. **Click** the left mouse button to set the cursor on the text box.

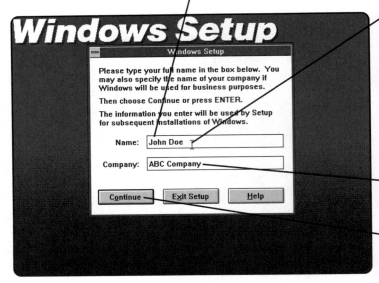

12. **Type** your **name**.

13. **Move** the mouse arrow to the **Company text box**. It will change to an I-beam.

14. **Click** on the **Company text box** to set the cursor.

15. **Type** your **company name** if appropriate.

16. **Press Enter** (or click on Continue) to go to the next screen.

**17. Press Enter** (or click on Continue) if the information is correct. (If the information is not correct, move the mouse arrow to change and click the left mouse button to return to the previous screen.)

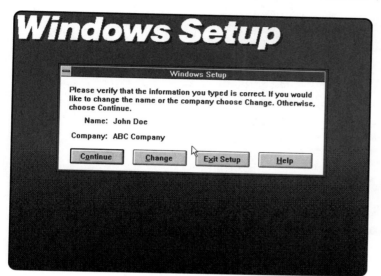

An empty Windows Setup screen followed by an hour-glass will appear briefly. Then the Windows Setup dialog box you see below will appear.

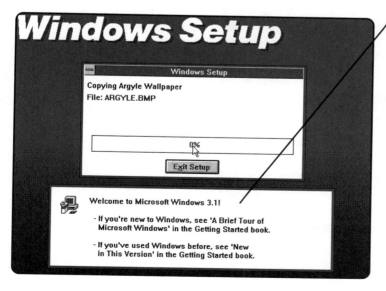

Once again Windows will show the progress of files being copied. When Disk #3 is copied, you will hear a beep. You will be asked to insert the next disk.

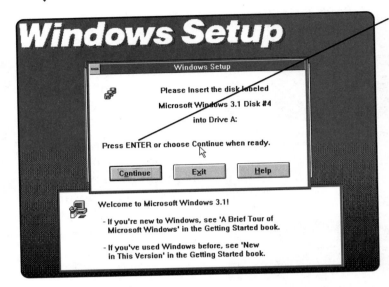

18. **Insert Disk #4** and **press Enter**. You will see the Setup progress screen. When Disk #4 is copied you will hear a beep. You will be asked to insert the next disk. This process will be repeated for Disk #5 and Disk #6.

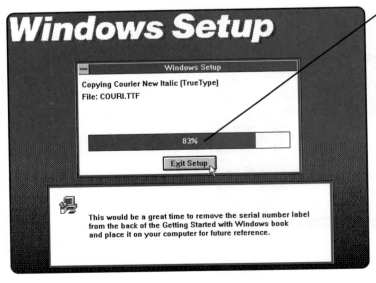

Windows will continue to show you the progress of files being copied as it copies Disks #5 and #6. It will beep when it finishes copying each disk.

## FIRST-TIME INSTALLATION

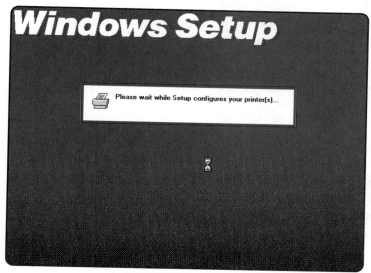

If this is a first-time installation of Windows you will be asked for additional information about your printer.

**Insert** the **disk asked for** and **press Enter**. The directions are detailed in the section "Installing a Printer" on the next page.

Also, after installing the printer, you may be asked to install DOS applications. See the section on "Installing DOS Applications" on page 252.

## UPGRADE INSTALLATION

If this is an upgrade installation and Windows has a newer driver for your printer, you will be asked for additional information. **Insert** the **disk asked for** and **press Enter**. Follow the directions in the section, "Installing Printers," on the next page.

From this point on, the sequence of screens may be different from what is shown in the rest of this chapter. It will depend on:

❖ The type of system you have

❖ The printers that need to be installed

❖ The DOS programs you may or may not want to set up for Windows. The final installation screens are illustrated on the following pages.

# INSTALLING A PRINTER

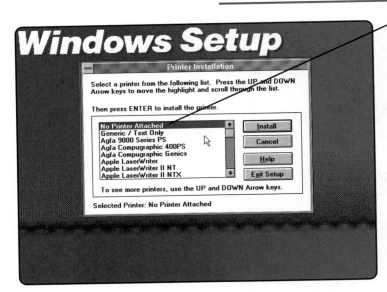

1. **Press and hold** the **Down Arrow** key on your **keyboard** until the highlight bar selects the name of your printer (or the printer that your printer emulates).

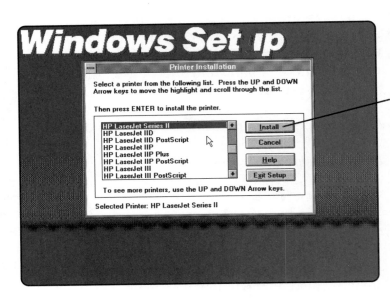

This example shows the HP LaserJet Series II highlighted.

2. **Press Enter** (or click on Install). Another Printer Installation dialog box will appear.

3. **Press** the **Down Arrow key** on your **keyboard** to move the highlight bar to the communication port to which your printer is connected. Most printers are connected to the LPT1 port. If you're not sure which one to select, choose LPT1. If your printer doesn't work after this installation, see Chapter 12, "Changing Your Primary Printer," and Chapter 13, "Basic Printer Settings."

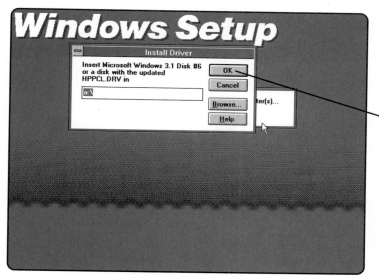

4. **Press Enter** (or click on Install). The Install Driver dialog box will appear.

In this example, the dialog box asks you to insert Windows 3.1 Disk #6. Depending on your printer, you may be asked to insert a different numbered disk.

5. **Insert** the appropriate **disk** in **drive A**.

6. **Press Enter** (or click on OK). The printer you chose is now installed.

# INSTALLING DOS APPLICATIONS

You may be asked to identify the DOS applications on your computer by name so that Windows can set them up to work in the new version.

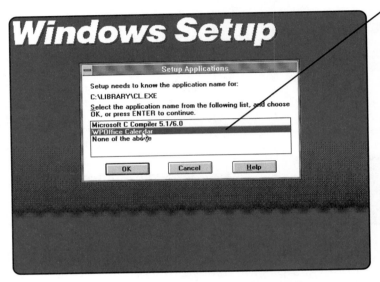

1. **Press** the **Down Arrow key** on your **keyboard** to move the highlight bar to the name of the application you want to set up. In this example, we highlighted WPOffice Calendar.

2. **Press Enter**. Windows will now set this program up. You may have to interact with additional screens depending on what software you have installed on your computer. For more on setting up DOS programs, see Chapter 6, the section entitled "Method #1: Search for Applications."

If you are upgrading, the Setup Applications dialog box to the left asks about the PIF files that your previous version of Windows has created (if any).

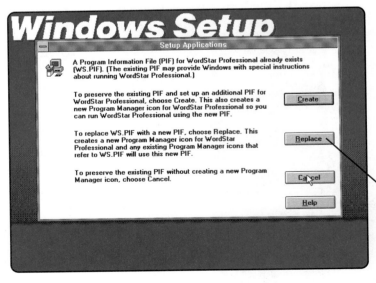

3. **Move** mouse arrow to the **Replace button** and **press Enter**. You may be asked to interact with more than one screen like this one. For more on setting up DOS programs, see Chapter 6, the section entitled, "Method #3: The PIF Editor."

# COMPLETING THE INSTALLATION

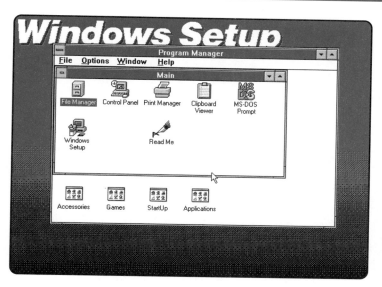

When the Windows installation is almost complete, you will see the Program Manager window for a short time. Another window, such as the Main group window, may also be open. You may also see a screen that asks you if you want to do the Windows tutorial. Regardless of whether or not you elect to do the tutorial at this time, your final installation screen will look like the one at the bottom of this page.

1. **Remove** any floppy **disks** from your drive.

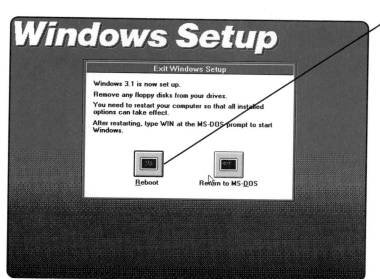

2. **Press Enter** (or click on Reboot). Windows will reboot your computer and then boot itself up.

Congratulations! You have successfully installed Windows 3.1 on your computer.

# Starting Windows Mouse Tutorial

Windows provides an excellent animated tutorial on using the mouse. This appendix will tell you how to start the tutorial program. You must have Windows 3.1 installed on your computer to use the tutorial. If you don't, see Appendix A, "Installing for First-Time and Upgrade Users."

## BOOTING UP THE MOUSE TUTORIAL

1. When you are at the DOS prompt (C:\>), **type win** and **press Enter**. This will boot up Windows.

When Windows boots up, you will see the Program Manager window on your screen.

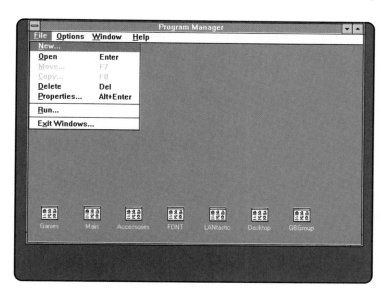

2. **Press and hold** the **Alt** key. At the same time, **type** the letter **f** (Alt + f). A pull-down menu will appear.

This is the way to open the File pull-down menu using only the keyboard.

3. **Type** the letter **r**. The Run dialog box will appear.

4. **Type** the following in the Command Line text box:

**c:\windows\wintutor.exe**

This will boot up the Microsoft Windows 3.1 Tutorial program.

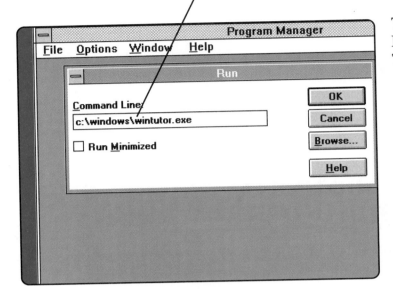

5. Follow the directions on the screen. The tutorial will take you through all the steps you need to know.

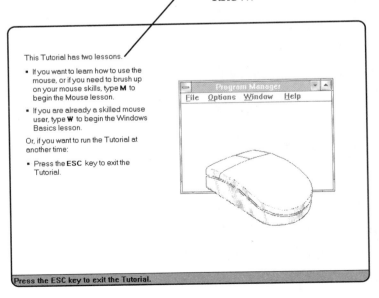

# Index

# R

Random single files, selection of, 191
Replacing text in Windows Write, 209
Resizing program windows, 28-29
Resolution of printer, setting of, 147-148
Restore button, 8, 9
    and disappearing icons, 37
Restoring windows, 8, 9
Right Align in Windows Write, 204
Right and left mouse buttons,
    switching of, 135-136
Root directory, 79
Ruler line, 203
    tab-setting with, 205

# S

Save As command, 213
Save Settings on Exit, 75
Saving. *See also* Backing up
    desktop as customized, 74-75
    documents in Windows Write, 212-
        213
    icon changes, 100
    Notepad files, 224-225
    in working directory, 87-88
Screen saver
    customizing of, 124-125
    Desktop dialog box for, 121-122
    pattern, selection of, 123
Scroll bars, 11
Scroll down arrow, 12
Scrolling, 11
    to any position, 15
    one line at a time, 12-13
    rapid scrolling, 14

Scroll left arrow, 13
Scroll right arrow, 13
Scroll up arrow, 12
Search for Applications method, 51
    automatic setups and, 55
    use of, 55-62
Search Now, 56
Second program, switching to, 24-25
Seconds for Clock, 233
Selecting files, 190-191
Selecting goals, xvii-xxi
Setup dialog box, 54-55
Setups
    advantages of methods of, 51-53
    automatic setup, 55-56
    closing windows setup, 58-59
    PIF editor, 67-71
    Search for Applications method, 55-
        62
    selecting DOS programs for, 57
    Specify an Application method, 63-
        66
Sideways printing, 163-164
Single spacing icon, 204
Size
    of program window, 28-29
    of window, 17-18
Sorting files, 188
Source diskette, 241
Specific file, booting to, 89-91
Specify an Application method, 52
    use of, 63-66
Speed
    double-click speed, 133-134
    mouse arrow speed, 133
    print speed, control of, 180
Spooling. *See* Print Manager
Starting Windows, 3
Startup feature, 92

# Be a POWER WINDOWS User!

Written in the same easy-to-understand style as this book,
the **I DO WINDOWS Newsletter**
is jammed full of *Hot Tips* guaranteed to be
easy to follow and easy to use.

Get product reviews, step-by-step directions and
answers to the most-asked questions.

◆ **Non-technical explanations**

◆ **All directions linked to graphic illustrations**

◆ **Easy-to-understand language**

◆ **Step-by-step directions detailing the easy
way to do power functions**

Complete the form and return it for a free copy of
I DO WINDOWS.
And, if you choose to subscibe today, you'll get
50% off the subscription price!

Offer expires December 31, 1992

6X per year / 8 pages per issue
3-hole punch paper

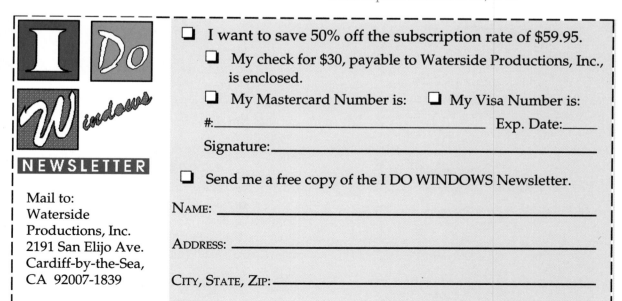